Test Your

Professional English

Management

In memory of Wicher Hento, 1938–2000, a valued friend and colleague, of Hogeschool Windesheim, Zwolle, Netherlands.

Pearson Education Limited
Edinburgh Gate
Harlow
Essex CM20 2JE, England
and Associated Companies throughout the world.

ISBN 0 582 46897 3
2nd impression, 2002
First published 2002
Text copyright © Simon Sweeney 2002

Designed and typeset by Pantek Arts Ltd, Maidstone, Kent
Test Your format devised by Peter Watcyn-Jones
Illustrations by David Eaton and Roger Fereday
Printed in Italy by Rotolito Lombarda

Acknowledgements
Thanks to colleagues and friends in the School of Management, Community and Communication at York St John College; to Steve Flinders of York Associates; also to my editor, Nick Brieger, for his usual patience and understanding. Helen Parker and Jane Durkin at Pearson Education also showed copious quantities of both these assets. They also suggested many useful improvements to the manuscript. Needless to say, whatever weaknesses remain are entirely my own responsibility.

Simon Sweeney

Published by Pearson Education Limited in association with Penguin Books Ltd, both companies being subsidiaries of Pearson plc.

For a complete list of the titles available from Penguin English please visit our website at www.penguinenglish.com, or write to your local Pearson Education office or to: Marketing Department, Penguin Longman Publishing, 80 Strand, London WC2R 0RL.

Contents

To the student

Do you use English in your work or in your studies? Perhaps you are already working in management. Or maybe you are a student doing a management course or a business studies programme. Perhaps you are planning to study a management degree, even an MBA. If you need to improve your knowledge of management and management terms, this book will help you. You can check your knowledge of basic management concepts, key words and essential expressions so that you can communicate more effectively and confidently in your work and for your studies.

There are eight sections in the book. The first section is a basic introduction to management functions, terms and concepts. The remaining seven sections each cover a different area of management including leadership and organizational culture, managing change and the external environment. You can either work through the book from beginning to end or select chapters according to your interests and needs.

Many tests also have useful tips (advice) on language learning or further professional information. The tips offer important extra help, especially as they introduce some additional key language.

Many different kinds of tests are used, including sentence transformation, gap-filling, word families, multiple choice, crosswords and short reading texts. There is a key at the back of the book so that you can check your answers, and a word list to help you revise key vocabulary.

Your vocabulary is an essential resource for effective communication. The more words you know, the more meanings you can express. This book will help you develop your specialist vocabulary still further. Using the tests you can check what you know and also learn new concepts and new words in a clearly structured framework.

Simon Sweeney

The full series consists of:

Test Your Professional English: Accounting	Alison Pohl
Test Your Professional English: Business General	Steve Flinders
Test Your Professional English: Business Intermediate	Steve Flinders
Test Your Professional English: Finance	Simon Sweeney
Test Your Professional English: Hotel and Catering	Alison Pohl
Test Your Professional English: Law	Nick Brieger
Test Your Professional English: Management	Simon Sweeney
Test Your Professional English: Marketing	Simon Sweeney
Test Your Professional English: Medical	Alison Pohl
Test Your Professional English: Secretarial	Alison Pohl

1 Job titles

Match the job title with the best definition on the right.

1	Chief Executive Officer (CEO)	a	Manager responsible for buying.
2	Information Systems Director	b	Person who designs computer networks.
3	Purchasing Director	c	British English term for senior manager of a company.
4	Human Resources Director	d	Manager responsible for the process of creating goods or services for sale to customers.
5	Systems Analyst	e	American English term for the top manager of a company.
6	Managing Director	f	Person responsible for setting up training opportunities for employees.
7	Marketing Director	g	The person responsible for computer operations in a company.
8	Production Director	h	Person responsible for managing product development, promotion, customer service, and selling.
9	Customer Service Manager	i	Person responsible for markets in other countries.
10	Staff Development Officer	j	Manager responsible for personnel issues.
11	Finance Director	k	Person responsible for relationships with customers.
12	Exports Manager	l	Person responsible for presentation and control of profit and loss.

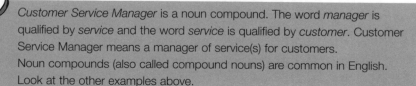

Customer Service Manager is a noun compound. The word *manager* is qualified by *service* and the word *service* is qualified by *customer*. Customer Service Manager means a manager of service(s) for customers.
Noun compounds (also called compound nouns) are common in English. Look at the other examples above.

2 The role of managers

The table shows four main roles of managers: planning, organizing, leading and controlling. Below the table is a list of management functions. Write each function under the correct heading.

Planning	Organizing
taking on new staff	

Leading	Controlling

Management functions

communicating with staff   comparing results with targets

deciding strategy   empowering staff to take decisions

identifying change   identifying needs   managing resources

monitoring quality standards   motivation

putting systems in place   setting objectives   ~~taking on new staff~~

team-building supervision   time management

 Peters and Waterman (1982) say that planning, organizing, influencing and controlling are critical **management functions** that should be characterized by a bias for action.

3 Defining management

Here are some definitions of management and the role of managers. Complete the sentences with words from the box.

---

assembling   controlling   financial (x2)   goals   human (x2)   information
innovation (x2)   leadership   leading   marketing   material (x2)
organization (x2)   organizing   planning (x2)   process (x2)   resources (x2)

---

1   Managers are responsible for 'the p r o c e s s of p _ _ _ _ _ _ _,
o _ _ _ _ _ _ _ _ _, l _ _ _ _ _ _ and c _ _ _ _ _ _ _ _ _ the efforts
of o _ _ _ _ _ _ _ _ _ _ members and of using all organizational
r _ _ _ _ _ _ _ _ to achieve stated organizational g _ _ _ _'.
(Mescon, Albert and Khedourie, 1985, quoted in Hannagan, 1998, p.4)

2   '(Management is) getting things done by other people'.
(Mary Parker Follett, 1941, quoted in Hannagan, 1998, p.4)

3   '(Management is) the process of optimizing h _ _ _ _,
m _ _ _ _ _ _ _ and f _ _ _ _ _ _ _ _ contributions for the
achievement of organizational goals'.
(Pearce and Robinson, 1989, quoted in Hannagan, 1998, p.4)

4   A modern view of management, expressed by Sir Roland Smith,
is that 'Management should be based on i _ _ _ _ _ _ _ _ _,
m _ _ _ _ _ _ _ _ and risk'.
(quoted in Hannagan 1998, p.5)

5   'All managers may be involved with the operational aspects of
management but as they are promoted and develop, their role
becomes increasingly one of p _ _ _ _ _ _ _, i _ _ _ _ _ _ _ _ _
and l _ _ _ _ _ _ _ _ _'.
(Hannagan, 1998, p.5)

6   Management is 'the _ _ _ _ _ _ _ of a _ _ _ _ _ _ _ _ _ and using
r _ _ _ _ _ _ _ _ _ – h _ _ _ _, f _ _ _ _ _ _ _ _ and m _ _ _ _ _ _ _, and
i _ _ _ _ _ _ _ _ _ _ _ – in a goal-directed manner to accomplish tasks
in an o _ _ _ _ _ _ _ _ _ _ _ _'.
(Black and Porter, 2000, p.19)

4 Characteristics of managers

Match each term in the box with the pictures (1–12).

creative   ~~emotionally strong~~   flexible   good communicator   knowledgeable   leadership skills   mental skills   sensitive to others   social skills   technically skilled

1 *emotionally strong*

2 _____

3 _____

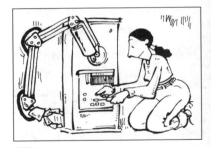

4 _____

5 _____

6 _____

7 _____

8 _____

9 _____

10 _____

Adjectives are often formed with suffixes (endings) added to the root of a word. Look at the endings in the following adjectives from the list above:

creat**ive**

flex**ible**

knowledge**able**

sensit**ive**

skill**ed**

5 History of management theory

Below is a list of management theories over the last five hundred years. In each pair decide which statement is true.

1   Machiavelli *The Prince* (1513)

(a)) You have to be cleverer than your opponent, sometimes using force or trickery.

b) You have to kill your opponents.

2   Marx and Engels *The Communist Manifesto* (1848)

a) The Communist Party will dominate the world.

b) The working class will rise up and take power from the bourgeoisie, creating a utopia of equality and brotherhood.

3   Taylorism (1911)

a) A 'scientific' approach to management based on measuring time, performance and output and relating these to wages and salaries.

b) A system of management based on friendly co-operation between managers and workers.

4   Hawthorne studies (1924–32)

a) Studies showing that factories produce more if workers are put under increased pressure.

b) Studies showing the relationships between management and workers are very important in getting the best performance.

5 Elton Mayo (1930s)

a) The idea that social needs and relationships are very important factors in the workplace.

b) The belief that workers should be able to control the work environment.

6 Maslow's Hierarchy of Needs (1942)

a) The idea that people have needs which motivate their performance. Once a need is met, it is no longer motivating.

b) The idea that workers and managers have the same needs and have to co-operate.

7 Systems approach (1950s and 60s)

a) Belief that organizations consist of many parts and management has to help each part to work both individually and as part of the whole organization.

b) Belief that a company is a single organization. Managing the single organization from the top brings success.

8 Contingency theory (1980s and after)

a) Idea that organizations are all similar and have the same objective – profit.

b) Management must study every situation and design the best response.

6 Marketing

Marketing is in many ways the central activity in business management. In commercial organizations, marketing is 'everybody's business'.

A Complete the definitions of marketing using words from the box.

demand	everything	people	promoting	services	~~things~~

1. Selling ____*things*____ that don't come back to _____ who do.

2. _____ a company does to influence _____ for its products and services.

3. _____ and selling goods and _____.

- A key concept in marketing is **Unique Selling Proposition (USP)**, the special qualities of a product or service. These qualities make the product different from competitor products and give it special appeal to consumers. Marketers aim to create a USP in their products.

- See also: Test 39 SWOT analysis.

B The Four Ps of marketing are now the Seven Ps, because of the increasing importance of services and customer service. Fill in the spaces below to match the seven Ps to the best definition.

People	Physical evidence	Place	Price
Process	~~Product~~	Promotion	

The traditional Four Ps are:

1 *Product*   The goods or services a company provides.

2 P _____   Decisions about what customers pay for the product.

3 P _____   Things concerned with location and distribution.

4 P _____   Ways to make the company and its products well known and ways to sell products.

And here are three more:

5 P _____   Everyone involved with the company and its products, especially the customers.

6 P _____   All the ways in which the company and its customers interact.

7 P _____   Anything that shows or mentions the name and image of the company and its products.

7 Management style

The table below contrasts two styles of behaviour, Culture A and Culture B. Study the table, then answer the True/False questions below.

Culture A	Managerial activity	Culture B
Plan for every situation. Develop plan *with* boss.	PLANNING	Accept surprises. Develop a plan, then ask boss to agree.
Create a department hierarchy. Communicate frequently face-to-face, rarely by e-mail.	ORGANIZING	Organize department into teams. Communicate infrequently face-to-face, often by e-mail.
Inform subordinates of decisions. Get involved in disputes between subordinates.	LEADING	Involve subordinates in decision-making. Allow subordinates to solve their own problems.
Monitor activities, guide behaviour. Emphasize financial results in evaluating performance.	CONTROLLING	Evaluate then reward – based on results. Focus on customer satisfaction in evaluation.

(Adapted from Black and Porter, 2000, p.102)

1   Culture A is more modern.   True/**False**

2   Culture A is more flexible.   True/False

3   In Culture A, the manager is more 'hands on' and
    directive.   True/False

4   Hierarchical companies have a top-down way of working.   True/False

5   Subordinates help in decision-making in less
    traditional, modern companies.   True/False

6   If finance is the main factor in decision-making,
    staff are happy.   True/False

 See also: Test 9 Theory X and Theory Y

8 Modern management theory

Complete the text below with the correct headings from the box.

> Corporate downsizing   Empowerment   ~~Just-In-Time~~
> Learning organizations   Outsourcing   Re-engineering
> Teamworking   Total Quality Management

1   Just-In-Time

This system was introduced from Japan in the 1980s. It means ordering components exactly when you need them, and supplying goods exactly when the customer needs them. It eliminates storage time and reduces costs.

2

Many large corporations and multi-nationals had grown too complex by the 1990s. Some sectors of the organization were less profitable. Many of these companies sold off or closed the under-performing sectors.

3

Management increasingly understands the value of sharing power with others throughout the organization. This leads to more participation in decision-making.

4

This is closely related to (3). By encouraging employees to work in very fluid teams, responsibility is shared. Employees and managers at all levels develop a better self-identity and work becomes more interesting. This system is seen as much more efficient than linear or hierarchical structures.

5

This is a total revision and restructuring of an entire company. It involves asking fundamental questions about the objectives of the business and how it operates. It aims to create big improvements in cost, quality, service and product.

6

This management approach focuses on measuring the quality of service in all aspects. The idea is to develop systems that are more efficient and more economical, but which are also more able to meet the needs of customers.

7

This approach recognizes that companies cannot do everything. It can be better to use external suppliers for some specialist operations, or particular components in manufacturing. This decision can create quality improvements and cost savings.

8

Many companies have developed internal training programmes to help with staff development. This is an important investment in the workforce. It not only makes people better at their job, but it also makes them happier. It may also help companies to keep their best managers and staff.

A key management function described by Peters and Waterman (1982) involves going around looking, listening and thinking about what is going on. They call it **Managing By Walking Around (MBWA).**

9 Theory X and Theory Y

What do managers think of their staff? McGregor (1960) said there were two opposing views, Theory X and Theory Y.

A Read the text below, then answer the True/False questions.

Theory X managers believe that people dislike work. Work is necessary because if you do not work you cannot live. People are naturally lazy. They prefer to be directed. So managers have to tell their subordinates what to do. Managers have to organize the workers and pressure them to do things. The manager's job is to think about the goals of the organization then make workers realize the goals. Subordinates want security. They want managers to organize and control everything. So Theory X managers are authoritarian. Managers are the bosses. They decide the goals and give orders. They direct everything, from the top down.

Theory Y is more or less opposite to Theory X.
Theory Y managers believe that people like work. Work is necessary because people want to work to feel happy. People are naturally industrious. They prefer to participate in decision-making. Managers discuss with their subordinates what to do. Managers organize communication channels with the workers and listen to their opinions. The manager's job is to establish the goals of the organization with the workers, so that together they can realize the goals. Subordinates want managers to involve them, to delegate decision-making, to allow them autonomy. Theory Y managers are team-oriented. They trust their subordinates. The organization is less hierarchical and more creative.

1 Theory X and Theory Y are theories of leadership. (True)/False

2 Theory X is a more traditional description of management/worker relations. True/False

3 Theory Y is typical in hierarchical top-down organizations. True/False

4   Theory Y managers tell workers what they want.
Workers do it.   True/False

5   Theory X managers are authoritarian.   True/False

6   Theory Y workers are lazy and don't want to work.   True/False

7   For Theory X workers, work is natural.   True/False

8   Theory Y working relationships are open,
communicative and creative.   True/False

B   Put the words and phrases below into the correct column.

> ~~communication~~   control   co-operation   creativity
> direction   modern   orders   participation   security
> traditional   work is a necessity   work is natural

Theory X	Theory Y
_____	*communication*
_____	_____
_____	_____
_____	_____
_____	_____
_____	_____

- Leadership is one aspect of management. Good managers often have some of the characteristics of good leaders.
- See also: Test 7 Management style

10 Leadership styles

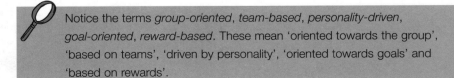

Tick the *three* words or phrases that match each style of leadership.

1 Autocratic leadership

open   modern   directive✓   hierarchical✓   creative   traditional✓

2 Democratic leadership

group-oriented   Communist   team-based   communicative
simple   charismatic

3 Laissez-faire leadership

open   non-existent   co-operative   creative   strong   modern

4 Charismatic leadership

political   personality-driven   goal-oriented   inspirational
bureaucratic   reward-based

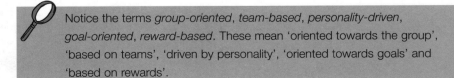

Notice the terms *group-oriented*, *team-based*, *personality-driven*,
goal-oriented, *reward-based*. These mean 'oriented towards the group',
'based on teams', 'driven by personality', 'oriented towards goals' and
'based on rewards'.

11 Team-building

Look at the diagram below. It shows that an effective team contains different people with different roles and different qualities. Study the diagram, then read the text that follows and fill in the spaces.

Balancing roles in an effective team

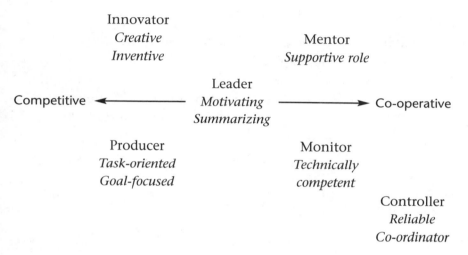

Innovator
Creative
Inventive

Mentor
Supportive role

Leader
Motivating
Summarizing

Competitive ◄————————— ————————► Co-operative

Producer
Task-oriented
Goal-focused

Monitor
Technically
competent

Controller
Reliable
Co-ordinator

Team-building: getting the balance right

The whole point of teamwork is that people work together. The most effective teams contain a balance of different people with different skills. For example, a team needs (1) ___**innovators**___ . These are creative, ideas-oriented people. They look for new solutions and explore alternatives. The team also needs (2) _____, people who get results. These are task-oriented and understand the objectives of the team. Both these types tend to be competitive.

Balancing this are more co-operative individuals. These may include (3) _____, who support team members and make sure good relationships are maintained. Others are (4) _____, with technical expertise and the ability to check progress, measure performance and ensure that things are both possible and desirable.

Another important role is the (5) _____, who works on all levels of co-ordination and organization of the team.

At the heart of the team is the (6) _____ . His/her role is to make sure that all parts of the team work well together. He/she must motivate team members to achieve the agreed objectives. He/she is also responsible for summarizing and reporting the work of the team.

Team building in the workplace creates a sense of *collective responsibility*. Everyone shares in success, everyone learns from mistakes, everyone works together to help everyone else. The result is – in theory – more harmony, less competition; more support, less isolation; more job satisfaction and lower turnover of staff. The combined result is more success.

12 Conflict management

A Conflict, like change, happens. There are different types of conflict in management contexts. Look at the table below and match the type of conflict (1–5) with the best definition (a–e).

Conflict type

1 Inter-group conflict

2 Intra-group conflict

3 Relationship conflict

4 Inertia

5 Substantive conflict

Definition

a Personality or inter-personal differences within a group.

b Conflict between groups.

c Disagreement on ideas or what to do.

d Conflict within a group.

e Failure to act or produce results.

B Below are five possible solutions to conflict. Complete the phrases using words from the box.

> communication skills   leader   mediator   methods   options

1 Redefine goals or working _____

2 Compare and evaluate _____

3 Appoint a _____

4 Improve _____

5 The _____ should intervene (or resign to allow a new leader to take over).

Notice the meaning of:

inter-   between

intra-   within

So the **Internet** is a network between different computers; an **intranet** is a network within one organization.

13 Motivation

A Complete the three definitions of motivation with words from the box.

behaves	~~drives~~	effort	outcomes	reach	willingness

- Motivation is what (1) ___*drives*___ us to try to (2) _____ certain goals.

- Motivation is a decision-making process through which a person chooses desired (3) _____ and (4) _____ in ways that will lead to acquiring them.

- Motivation is the (5) _____ to make the (6) _____ to achieve certain goals.

B An important theory of motivation in management is Maslow's Hierarchy of Needs. Maslow (1942) described five levels of need. Look at the pyramid below which shows these needs. Read the text on page 19 and write the names for each level (1–5) in the pyramid. Use the words in the box opposite.

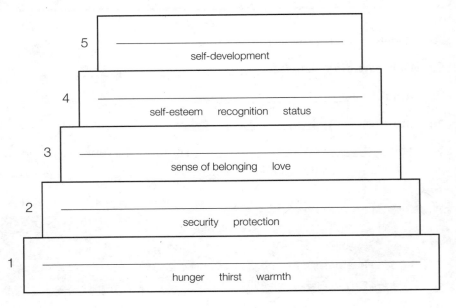

5 _____
self-development

4 _____
self-esteem   recognition   status

3 _____
sense of belonging   love

2 _____
security   protection

1 _____
hunger   thirst   warmth

> Esteem needs   Physiological needs   Safety needs
>
> Self-actualization   Social needs

Maslow's theory suggests that people treat each level as a motivating factor, but once a level is achieved it is no longer motivating. Instead, the next level up becomes the new motivator. This tells us that in the workplace, esteem needs are important, but once achieved, they are no longer significant. Self-actualization, or self-development, is much more important. Managers therefore have to make sure that their staff continually feel that they are improving and achieving more in terms of self-actualization.

Maslow also states that it is not possible to move up a step without first fulfilling the lower needs.

 Need is a verb. *Need* is also used as a singular noun, but most frequently it is used in the plural, *needs*.

Notice the prepositions in these phrases: *the need for (something), in need of (something), the needs of (someone)*.

Notice also the noun phrases *customer needs, financial needs, research needs, training needs*.

14 Negotiating styles

The text opposite describes three negotiating styles. Read it and then complete the table that follows.

Principled negotiation (win/win)

Creative negotiation

Adversarial negotiation (win/lose)

Most people negotiate to gain some advantage to themselves or to their side. The fighter is only interested in his side winning and the other side losing. This is a hard style of negotiation and involves making demands.

In business, it is often better to negotiate to independent advantage. This means each side thinks about its advantages, but knows that the result will bring either common benefits or different advantages to each side. Both sides get something and are happy with the result. In this type of negotiation everyone makes concessions. This is sometimes called a win/win negotiation. Another style of negotiation is seen in the creative negotiator. Here both sides look for agreement. Agreement is the main objective and one or both negotiators have a soft negotiating style.

Negotiation styles: a continuum

Adversarial negotiation	Principled negotiation	Creative negotiation
Negotiate to (1) _win_	Look for (2) _____ benefits	Look for (3) _____
Make (4) _____	Make (5) _____	Accept what is on offer
(6) F_____	Negotiator for independent and mutual advantages	(7) C_____ negotiator
(8)_____	Win/win	Agree

 See also: Test 37 Resistance to change

15 Project management

A   The following are typical stages in project management. Key words have been scrambled. Unscramble them.

1   Set <u>jobsevteic</u>   *objectives*

2   Establish <u>sonnifitide</u>

3   Appoint project <u>reelad</u> and <u>smeat</u>

4   Estimate <u>stocs</u> and provide a <u>dubteg</u>

5   Put work out to <u>redent</u>

6   Discuss <u>sopalrops</u>

7   <u>atetongie</u> with tendering companies

8   Sign <u>tontscrac</u>

9   <u>nalp</u> and <u>ledushec</u> the work

10   Provide necessary <u>trupsop</u>

11   <u>romiton</u> the work in progress

12   Evaluate <u>lessrut</u>

B   Match each of the words you have unscrambled with a word or phrase below that has a similar meaning.

For example: **1** *objectives*   **l** *aims*

a discuss	**f** offers	**k** assistance
b terms	**g** submissions	**l** aims
c organize	**h** check	**m** outcomes
d co-ordinator	**i** groups	**n** expenses
e set time targets	**j** agreements	**o** financial plan

16 Time management

Good time management is very important in an efficient workplace. Most people could improve their time management skills. Match an action (1–5) with its meaning (A–E) and an example (v–z).

Action	Meaning	Example
1 plan	**A** improve your abilities	**v** A colleague asks you to go to a meeting – but it is not absolutely necessary. You make an excuse and do not go.
2 delegate	**B** organize	**w** You write appointments, deadlines and actions in your diary. You know what you have to do for the week.
3 upgrade skills	**C** order things according to importance	**x** A new project has to be carried out. You do not have time to run it. You ask someone else to do it.
4 prioritize	**D** say no	**y** You decide that writing a report for your boss is the most important job today. Do that, then do something else that is urgent, but less important.
5 turn down requests	**E** get somebody else to do something	**z** You sign up for an in-service training seminar on Time Management.

How is your time management? Here are eight tips on time management: keep a diary; write weekly (or daily) *To Do* lists; prioritize; set objectives; make deadlines; act or delegate; build in relaxation time; and get enough sleep!

17 Defining organizatonal culture

A Every organization, every business, has its particular culture. Organizational culture combines aspects of an organization with its particular culture. Label each of the following as part of 'organization' (O) or as part of 'culture' (C).

1	Values	*C*
2	Having a clear structure	____
3	Beliefs	____
4	Formal sources of authority	____
5	Assumptions and attitudes	____
6	Norms	____
7	Objectives/Common purpose	____
8	Relationship between centre and periphery	____
9	Shared experience	____
10	The system	____

B Complete the dialogue below using words in part A.

A: How is organizational c u l t u r e created? What is it?

B: Organizational culture is a set of basic a _ _ _ _ _ _ _ _ _ _ , or what people think, in a company or organization.

A: So it's based on common v _ _ _ _ _?

B: That's right. Everyone learns these over time. They learn the way of doing things, the n _ _ _ _ .

A: And everyone agrees that they are right?

B: Generally, yes.

A: And where do they come from?

B: From shared experience. From history, tradition and common b _ _ _ _ _ _ .

A: And new employees usually learn the same things? They learn the s _ _ _ _ _ .

B: Exactly. Everyone learns the same organizational culture.

18 Characteristics of organizational culture

Company A and Company B have broadly **opposite** organizational cultures. For characteristics 1–6, fill in the spaces with a word which contrasts with the underlined word in the opposite column. For 7–10, complete the phrase so that it contrasts with the idea in the opposite column.

Company A	Company B
1 A <u>modern</u> manufacturing company.	A _traditional_ manufacturing company.
2 A f _ _ _ company structure.	A <u>hierarchical</u> company structure.
3 An <u>open</u> company with fluid communication channels.	A c _ _ _ _ _ company with clearly defined communication channels.
4 There are i _ _ _ _ _ _ _ meetings to decide policy.	There are <u>formal</u> meetings to explain policy.
5 There are <u>general guidelines</u> for employees to follow.	There are a lot of r _ _ _ _ and r _ _ _ _ _ _ _ _ _ _ for employees to follow.
6 The business is m _ _ _ _ _ -driven.	The business is <u>product</u>-driven.
7 Communication channels work in all directions, including sideways.	Communication channels are t _ _ - d _ _ _ .
8 Work is organized through a f _ _ _ _ _ _ _ system of teams, with a lot of exchange between teams.	Work is organized through a rigid system of d _ _ _ _ _ _ _ _ _ _ , with little exchange between them.
9 C _ _ _ _ _ _ _ _ _ , and innovative and dynamic work are highly valued.	Productivity and financial success are highly valued.
10 People are valued above s _ _ _ _ _ _ .	Systems are valued above p _ _ _ _ _ .

0134108950 7142

19 Developing organizational culture

Complete the sentences below (1–8) with a word from the word square. The words are all connected with things a company may use to develop its organizational culture.

R	I	M	K	S	Y	M	B	O	L	S
C	A	L	A	N	G	U	A	G	E	N
C	E	R	E	M	O	N	I	E	S	I
Z	A	H	N	Y	E	I	R	O	T	L
U	Y	E	O	T	Q	F	X	P	O	N
L	J	R	C	H	T	O	C	E	R	N
S	P	O	N	S	O	R	S	H	I	P
Z	A	E	P	D	K	M	F	G	E	W
H	I	S	L	N	S	S	T	T	S	U
M	A	G	A	Z	I	N	E	F	C	M
V	R	E	M	R	A	W	A	R	D	S

1   Many companies supply _u n i f o r m s_ for their employees which make them instantly recognizable and establish the idea of a team.

2   Many organizations and sectors of employment have a particular l _ _ _ _ _ _ _ with special words, special jargon unknown outside the business.

3   Many organizations have a special regular m _ _ _ _ _ _ _ full of news and comment on the activities of the organization.

4   Some organizations, especially those in leisure, sports and entertainment, use s _ _ _ _ _ _ _ _ _ _ to promote a particular image.

5   The history of many companies, and their boardrooms, are illustrated with pictures of company or organizational h _ _ _ _ _ .

6   Special prizes and a _ _ _ _ _ presented at special c _ _ _ _ _ _ _ _ _ help to build up the image of a company.

7   While fairy stories are not usually part of company history, there are s _ _ _ _ _ _ and sometimes m _ _ _ _ that become part of the organizational heritage.

8   Logos, letterheads, the painting on vehicles and on buildings, and all signs and s _ _ _ _ _ _ are a significant contribution to the culture of an organization.

20 Four dimensions of culture

Hofstede (1980) wrote about culture as 'collective programming' which affects behaviour. Here is a brief summary of Hofstede's work as applied to organizations. Complete the spaces using words from the box.

assertiveness	collective	competitiveness	~~dimensions~~
environment	femininity	individualism	masculine masculinity
power distance	subordinates	threat	uncertainty avoidance

What's your culture like?

Hofstede identified four (1) __dimensions__ of culture. These are power distance, uncertainty avoidance, individualism and masculinity.

The first, (2) p_____ d_____ , is a measure of inequality in organizations. It depends on management style, and reflects a measure of openness and effective communication between managers and (3) s _____ .

The second, (4) u_____ a_____, is a measure of how much people feel that new unusual situations are a (5) t_____.

(6) I_____ is a measure of how much the organization has an individualist or a (7) c _____ ethic.

The last one, (8) m _____ is contrasted with (9) f _____. This is a measure of how much the organization is assertive or competitive.

(10) A _____ and (11) c_____ are seen as (12) m _____ indicators. In contrast, caring and a stress on quality of life and concern for the (13) e_____ are seen as feminine characteristics.

21 Cultural variance

Trompenaars (1993) describes seven aspects of culture that affect behaviour. Below are five of these aspects which contain contrasting features, e.g. universal and particular, individual and collective, etc. Match each feature (1–10) with the correct meaning (a–j).

Aspects of culture

1	Universal
2	Particular
3	Individual
4	Collective
5	Neutral
6	Emotional
7	Diffuse
8	Specific
9	Achievement-based
10	Ascription-based

Meaning

a Business relationships are limited and contractual.

b Status, age, gender or education matter more than particular successes.

c Relationships are fluid and flexible depending on situation.

d Society is based on the whole community.

e People are reserved and do not easily express feelings.

f Recent or past successes are highly valued.

g The whole person is engaged in the business relationship and it takes time to build the relationship.

h Society is oriented towards individuals' wants and needs.

i Relatively rigid rule-based behaviour.

j It is common to express feelings openly.

- The other two aspects which Trompenaars describes are:

  Time: history and past experience, or current activities and potential to create the future

  Environment: the extent to which individuals affect the world they live in, or how much the world affects individuals

- See also: Test 59 Cultural issues

22 Power and politics

'A person can have power over you only if he or she controls something you desire.'

(Robbins, 1996, p.463)

A   Match the term on the left (1–6) with the best definition (a–f).

1	Referent power	a	Power that is based on fear.
2	Coercive power	b	The ability to make others do as you wish, because you control resources, e.g. favours, promotion or salary resources.
3	Reward power	c	The capacity that A has to influence B to do things he or she would not otherwise do.
4	Legitimate power	d	Power based on knowledge or special abilities.
5	Power	e	Influence that a person has because of special personality traits or desirable resources.
6	Expert power	f	Power that is based on status or position in an organization.

B Complete the following dialogue from a class on management with words from the box.

compromise	control	groups	influence	looking
	lose	~~organizational~~	status	

Student: What are (1) __*organizational*__ politics?

Tutor: They're the process by which individuals and
(2) _____ try to increase their
(3) _____ inside an organization.

Student: So being political can help you to have some
(4) _____ over aspects of your work?

Tutor: Exactly.

Student: What if you don't know the politics inside an organization?

Tutor: If you don't, you can (5) _____ power.

Student: So politicking means (6) _____ for influence then?

Tutor: Perhaps. In fact, a lot of the time you have to
(7) _____. But essentially the game is to raise
your (8)_____ within the organization.

23 How political are you?

Many political issues can affect the working environment. Match the issues (1–9) with the examples (a–i).

Issue	Example
1 Gender politics	**a** Saying a colleague has done a bad job, or made a mistake.
2 Equal opportunities	**b** Taking the opportunity to increase your power and influence because of someone else's weak position.
3 Ethics	**c** Treating everyone fairly, without considering their race, gender, beliefs, etc.
4 Peer competition	**d** Helping a colleague to do their job better.
5 Relationship-building	**e** Rivalry between colleagues for power, influence, opportunities and rewards.
6 Making alliances	**f** Creating shared attitudes and common views among a team.
7 Exploiting weakness	**g** Giving a woman a job because you need more women in that department.
8 Criticizing colleagues	**h** Creating common views with particular colleagues who have power and influence.
9 Giving friendly advice	**i** Making decisions about moral issues, such as the interests of the whole community.

Three of the above might **not** be acceptable in some contexts: saying a colleague has done a bad job, taking the opportunity to increase your power and influence *because of someone else's weakness*, and giving a woman a job because you need more women in a particular department.

24 The external environment

24 The external environment

Businesses and organizations have to adapt and respond to pressures from the external environment. The diagram shows eight kinds of pressure that impact on businesses. Match each one to an example (1–8) below

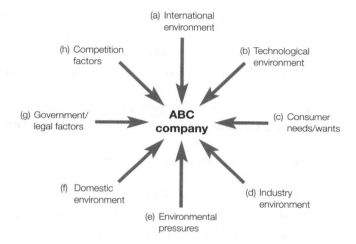

1   Other businesses offer similar or better products or services. __h__

2   Globalization offers opportunities to export more goods or services.

3   The target market changes because of demographic factors.

4   New laws affect product design.

5   Products become out-of-date due to new inventions.

6   Production costs increase because of difficulties in getting raw materials from ecologically sensitive areas, e.g. rain forests.

7   Changes in fashions among target markets.

8   The product is new and specialized and the market is growing.

 Word stress sometimes changes from the noun to the adjective. Look at the following:

technology   techno**log**ical   competition   com**pe**titive

industry   in**dus**trial   en**vi**ronment   environ**men**tal

25 The industry environment

This test looks at one of the eight external factors mentioned in Test 24. The *industry environment* means the industry in which a company works and all the factors which affect competition in that sector.

A Mark the following statements as True or False.

1 In an industrial sector with a low profit environment
it is impossible for a company to make large profits.   True/False

2 In an industrial sector with a high profit environment
there is usually a lot of competition.   True/False

3 Substitutes are possible alternatives that customers
can choose.   True/False

4 An environment with fragmented customers means
that the customers cannot act together to make
producers lower their prices.   True/False

5 Highly technical products with high start-up costs
make it difficult for new producers to enter the market.   True/False

6 High quality and low price normally go together.   True/False

7 If there are many suppliers of a product, then the
suppliers are in a weak position. If there are few,
high profits are easier to obtain.   True/False

B The chart below shows the possible contrast between a high profit environment and a low profit environment. Complete the missing words. Note: The information in part A will help you to do this.

The industry environment and profit

Higher profits

- Q _ _ _ _ _ _ -based competition
- Few competitors
- Difficult m _ _ _ _ _ to enter
- Few new players in the market
- Few substitutes
- Many c _ _ _ _ _ _ _ _
- Many suppliers
- F _ _ _ _ _ _ _ _ _ customers

Lower profits

- Price-based competition
- Many c _ _ _ _ _ _ _ _ _ _
- Easy market to enter
- Many new players in the market
- Many s _ _ _ _ _ _ _ _ _ _
- Few customers
- Few s _ _ _ _ _ _ _ _
- United customers

Don't confuse the *industry environment* with the phrase *industrial marketing*. *Industrial marketing* means promoting and selling goods and services to organizations and industries, not primarily to consumers. *Industrial marketing* contrast with *consumer marketing*, where businesses market their goods mainly to private individuals.

26 Ethical issues 1

Match the ethical issue (1–10) with an example (a–j) and a picture (A–J) that illustrates the issue.

1 *g* H

Ethical issue		**Example**	
1	Workers' rights	a	Agreeing to set high prices with a competitor.
2	Animal rights	b	Not giving a job to someone because they are of a different ethnic origin.
3	Corruption	c	Marketing a dangerous product.
4	Computer data protection	d	Secretly giving money to a business partner to get a favour from him/her.
5	Codes of conduct	e	Putting dangerous chemicals into a river.
6	Company 'perks'	f	Testing products on rabbits.
7	Consumer safety	g	Making staff work very long hours.
8	Discrimination	h	Stealing secrets from a computer network.
9	Environmental protection	i	Giving *some* employees special benefits.
10	Operating a cartel	j	Getting drunk at lunchtime.

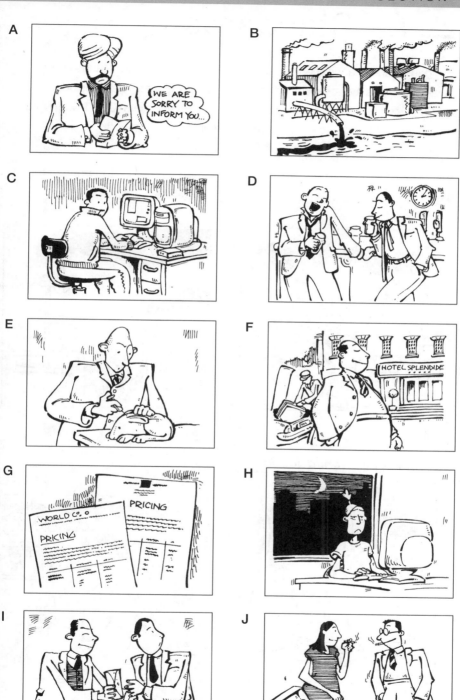

27 Standards

Companies and organizations need to meet certain minimum standards of behaviour. There are at least four categories of standards. These include standards of behaviour: towards customers and consumers (CC); towards the law (L); towards employees (E); towards the environment (ENV).

Look at the pictures below.

A Identify the category. Some are concerned with more than one category.

B Label each picture by unscrambling the words.

1 ___L, E___

hicld rabuol ___child labour___

2 _____

rai loptuloni _____

3 _____

konwirg donticoins _____

4 _____

rafud _____

5 _____

dofo dastarnds _____

7 _____

lois natoncimaniot _____

6 _____

libilriatey _____

8 _____

tefsya dasdranst _____

28 Looking after people: Health and Safety

Companies and organizations have a legal and moral responsibility to look after their employees and their customers. Health and Safety regulations protect employees. Consumer Protection laws protect consumers.

A   Label the pictures below with words from the box.

> air-conditioning   ergonomics   ~~product testing~~
>
> protective clothing   safety cap on a cleaning agent
>
> safety mask for a welder   vivisection   warning notice on a paint tin

1   *product testing*
     CP

2   _____

3   _____

4   _____

5 _____

_____

6 _____

_____

7 _____

_____

8 _____

_____

B Now label each of the above 'H&S' (health and safety provisions for staff), or 'CP' (consumer protection).

A noun compound consists of two nouns, e.g. *safety mask, paint tin, product testing*). These phrases typically mean the same as:

a mask for safety

a tin for paint

testing of products

Normally the first noun in the noun compound is in the singular, i.e. *product testing* not *products testing*.

29 Ethical issues 2

Below is a list of issues which may or may not create ethical dilemmas for a company or organization. Unscramble the underlined words.

1. Cigarette gadvisterin. _advertising_

2. puslime displays of sweets. _____

3. Animal tintseg of pharmaceutical products. _____

4. seviticoniv for cosmetics, soaps and shampoo products. _____

5. elswith-blowing to expose corruption in your organization. _____

6. Having no equal popsiteteruin policy in employment. _____

7. Changing jobs and taking fecdatilinon information on suppliers to your new job. _____

8. Presenting figts to a possible buyer. _____

9. Offering corporate toyasphilit to employees and their partners. _____

10. itronmoop of sweet drinks to children. _____

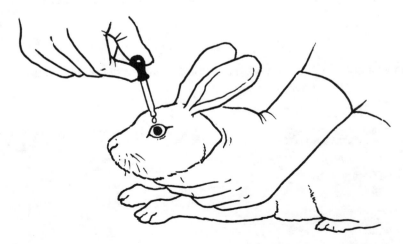

Testing products on animals is an ethical issue.

30 The legislative environment

Companies and organizations operate in a legal environment. Below are ten areas of legislation. Match each legislative area (1–10) with the correct description (a –j).

Legislative area

1	Environmental legislation
2	Social legislation
3	Consumer protection
4	Dangerous goods security legislation
5	Tariffs, duties and taxes
6	Official secrets, state security legislation
7	Sale of goods legislation
8	Company law
9	Advertising standards
10	Equal opportunities law

What is it about?

a	Minimum standards in quality, service and rights of customers.
b	Restrictions on use, movement and sale of items that present serious risk.
c	Protection of air, water and land.
d	Issues concerning state such as defence interests, nuclear resources, etc.
e	Employment law, hours of work, holidays, insurance, etc.
f	Restrictions on ways of promoting goods and services.
g	Compulsory levies applied by government.
h	Rights for all groups in society to be treated fairly.
i	The quality of goods and services and the accuracy of any claims made for products and services offered for sale.
j	Obligations to publish accounts, names of directors, etc.

The noun *goods* is only used in the plural and takes a plural verb, e.g. *The goods remain our property until payment is received in full.*

Other common plural noun forms are:

premises (buildings), *assets* (financial), *contents, funds, savings*

The singular form of these nouns has a different meaning from the plural form.

31 Forces for change

What are some of the most important forces for change? Match the pictures (1–10) with the forces for change (a–j).

1 _____j_____

2 _____

3 _____

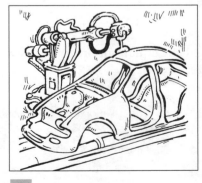

4 _____

5 _____

6 _____

7 _____

8 _____

9 _____

10 _____

a	legislative change	f	technological change
b	consumer needs and wants	g	competition
c	demographic change	h	automation
d	public opinion	i	environmental/ecological factors
e	changing leisure habits	j	changes in financial environment

> *The* **environment** means the world in which we live and work. The term is often used in connection with ecological concerns. We can describe a more specific environment by adding a qualifier, e.g. *the business environment, the competitive environment, the local environment, the political environment, the economic environment.*
>
> The word 'environment' is usually used in the singular, but notice the phrase *in different environments.*

32 The process of managing change

Change happens. Managing change is about dealing with this reality.
Complete the words in the diagram with words that mean the same – or
almost the same – as the words or phrases in the box.

1 say that something will happen	2 calculate	3 fix	4 design
5 carry out	6 check	7 evaluate	8 give a prize

PLANNING
(1)p _ _ _ _ _ _
change

RESEARCH
(2)a _ _ _ _ _
impact

(8)r _ _ _ _ _
success

EVALUATION
(7)m _ _ _ _ _ _
performance

COMMUNICATION
(3)s _ _ goals/
objectives

assess
and adapt
strategy

TRAINING
(4)p _ _ _ courses/
seminars

CHECKING/CONTROLLING
(6)m _ _ _ _ _ _
implementation and progress

ACTION
(5)i _ _ _ _ _ _ _ _
strategy

33 Innovation

Look at the graph, which shows five stages of innovation. Complete the description below with words from the box.

Five stages of innovation

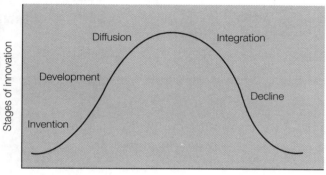

Time →

(Black and Porter, 2000, p.112)

decline	development	diffusion	~~innovation~~	integration
invention	inventor	market	patent	range

There are typically five stages of (1)__*innovation*__. First there is
(2) i_____, which means thinking of a new product or new idea.
During this period, the (3) i_____ should (4) p_____
the idea. Then the second phase is (5) d_____, where the idea is
adapted to the needs of a specific (6) m_____ . Then comes the
(7) d_____ stage, where the idea is sold and used by consumers.
Next the company fully accepts the innovation and it becomes a full part
of the business's product (8) r_____ . This phase is called
(9) i_____ . The final phase is called (10) d_____ .
Perhaps technology moves on or consumer demand changes and the idea
or product is no longer needed.

Compare the five stages of innovation with a classic **product life cycle**.
It is very similar. The product life cycle is often described in terms of
development, launch, growth, maturity, saturation, and decline.

34 Training

Training is a key aspect of dealing with change. Answer the questions below with words or phrases from the box.

curriculum vitae (CV)   graduate   human resources in-service training   lecture   qualification   research retraining   seminar   skills audit   staff development trainee   trainer   training budget   ~~training manager~~

1 What is the name of the person responsible for training in a company or organization? ___*training manager*___

2 What is a possible alternative to making an employee redundant? _____

3 What do you call a special award that is given after a training course? _____

4 What is the word to describe someone with a university degree? _____

5 What is the document that lists a person's work and educational experience? _____

6 What is the term for a special study to find out something? _____

7 What is the name of a process to find out the level of competence needed for certain activities, or the existing competence of staff? _____

8 What is the term used for the money available to spend on training? _____

9   Which department is usually responsible for training?

_____

10   What is the name for a single small conference or meeting, for discussion or training? _____

11   What is the term for making training available to staff?

_____

12   What is the name for a single talk given by an expert to a training group? _____

13   What do you call someone who trains staff?

_____

14   What do you call someone who is being trained?

_____

15   What is the term for training given to employees as part of their job? _____

The -ing form of the verb is called the gerund when it stands in place of a noun: training. Gerunds are common: engineering, teamworking, downsizing, outsourcing, data processing, marketing, etc.

35 Organizational change

'Adapt or die'. This is a common saying in business. Businesses and organizations must respond to change. Match the terms (1–8) with the correct definitions (a–h).

1	Organizational development	**a**	An approach to change that is based on looking at people and their relationships to the whole. The approach is planned, strategic and long-term.
2	Change agents	**b**	A concept of organizational change that is based on flexibility and continuous change.
3	Bench-marking	**c**	A combination of forces that do not want change.
4	Communication	**d**	Study of the impact of change.
5	Resistance to change	**e**	Radical redesign of all aspects of an organization's activities.
6	Re-engineering	**f**	Explaining why change is necessary and how it should happen.
7	Data analysis	**g**	A process of identifying a model of 'best practice' and comparing performance against this model.
8	Organizational renewal	**h**	People responsible for making change happen in organizations.

The prefix *re-* means 'to do something again'. Here are some words with the prefix that we have seen in this book:

- *re-engineering*
- *retraining*
- *redesign*
- *redefine*

re is used with a hyphen (*re-*) before 'e', e.g. *re-engineering*. We also use a hyphen if there is a similar word, in order to show the difference, e.g. *to re-form* (to form again) compared with *to reform* (to change).

36 Change and communication

A When managers have to introduce change, good communication is very important. There are many ways to communicate in businesses and organizations. Look at the definitions (1–8) and match them with ways to communicate in the box below. Do not use all the words in the box.

> company reports   departmental meeting   ~~discussion~~   e-mail
> extranet   fax   formal presentations   internal mail   Internet
> intranet   memos   newsletters   notice-board   post   quality circles
> teleconferencing   telephone   video-tape   voice-mail

1 Conversation about a particular topic.   ___*discussion*___

2 A method of using computer and TV monitor links to hold a meeting in real-time, but when the participants are in different places.   _____

3 Occasional meetings between colleagues to talk about how performance can be improved.   _____

4 A form of telephone answering system.   _____

5 Paper correspondence between employees in the same organization.   _____

6 Traditional letter correspondence.   _____

7 A private network accessible from PCs and open only to members of the same organization or group. Users can read and respond to messages posted on a website.   _____

8 A private network restricted to members of the same organization and authorized outsiders. Users can read and respond to messages posted on a website   _____

B Complete the table below with all the words from the box on page 51.

Written/printed communication	Speech communication	Machine communication
memos		

The virtual office has become a reality. Working from home, using networked computers and electronic data transfer (EDT), is now an alternative to the traditional office. **Mobile communications**, including cell phones that can send and receive **e-mail** messages, and laptop computers, mean you can have a portable office. **Video-conferencing** capabilities are improving all the time. **Electronic funds transfer (EFT)** and **home-shopping** using the **Internet** are everyday tools.

37 Resistance to change

Change is often met with resistance. Change agents therefore have to negotiate with those who would prefer to resist the changes. Complete the headings for the five stages of negotiation with words from the box.

---

agreement   concessions or compromise   information

persuasion   ~~planning~~   preparation   relationship building

---

Stage I

_____Planning_____ and _____

Before face-to-face meetings, the foundations have to be ready. Collect information. Decide on a strategy. Set objectives.

Stage II

_____ **between negotiating parties**

This stage is about developing trust between the parties.

Stage III

_____ **exchange**

Learn about the needs and demands of the other side.

Stage IV

_____ **attempts**

Attempts to modify the position of the other side. Negotiation is about increasing the influence of your side.

Stage V

_____ **and** _____

In this stage both sides make changes in their original position. If this happens, both sides leave the negotiation with some satisfaction.

- Note the verb phrases
  to make a concession
  to make concessions
  to agree/make a compromise
  to make compromises
  to compromise
- See also: Test 14 Negotiating styles

38 Planning

All the words in the box concern planning. Match each term with the correct definition (1–12). The answers include the word *plan* eight times.

---

action   budget   business   contingency
interim   objectives   operational   planning provisional
~~strategic~~   tactical

---

1 A plan that focuses on the whole organization, internal and external factors, and actions necessary to reach long-term goals.
_____*strategic plan*_____

2 A process that focuses on the future of an organization and how to reach certain targets. _____

3 The results or targets that management thinks are desirable._____

4 A plan for a specific part of the wider organization, usually narrower in scope and over a shorter time period.
_____

5 A specific short-term plan to realize a narrow single objective.
_____

6 A short-term and temporary plan. _____

7 A trial plan, that may or may not be adopted permanently.
_____

8 A plan which explains a new commercial activity or new company and how to start it. _____

9 A plan of what to do, often indicating individual responsibilities, often short-term. _____

10 A plan which sets out the forecast costs of a project or activity.
_____

11 A reserve plan which will only be used if necessary.
_____

39 SWOT analysis

A classic way to create a marketing strategy is to begin by looking at a company's Strengths, Weaknesses, Opportunities and Threats. Expo Marketing Consultants carried out a SWOT analysis of GUBU Toys Ltd. Put all their findings in the correct box to complete the SWOT analysis.

1	Reliable and committed workforce
2	Use of wood – seen as 'good for the environment'
3	High labour costs
4	Location – far from population centres/far from new markets
5	Beautiful handmade toys
6	Poor communications systems / limited technological skills
7	Internet as potential marketing tool / e-commerce
8	Lack of IT training in staff
9	Declining interest in domestic markets for traditional toys
10	Potentially strong demand in Germany and Scandinavia
11	Competition in Germany and Scandinavia / Baltic countries
12	Increased competition from mail order companies
13	Selling by new channels, e.g. mail order

Expo Marketing Consultants SWOT Analysis for GUBU (Toys) Ltd	
Strengths *1*	**Weaknesses**
Opportunities 	**Threats**

- Strengths and Weaknesses are concerned with things **inside** the company which it can directly control. Opportunities and Threats are **outside** factors.
- See also: Test 6 Marketing

40 The business plan

Read the text below on preparing a business plan. Then look at the Contents page from the Business Plan of Gorliz & Zimmerman, an office furniture manufacturer. Complete the missing words.

Preparing a Business Plan

The business plan is an important document with two essential functions. It aims to convince possible investors and other stakeholders of the potential of a new business. It also works as a guide for the company in its first year or two of operation.

The business plan normally starts with a title page and outline of the new business. It includes the name, logo and mission statement of the activity. There are normally three main parts to the business plan.

First, the Marketing Plan. This includes a description of the products and services, an analysis of the market, a survey of the competition and a basic outline of promotion and selling strategies.

The next part is the Financial Plan, which includes details of start-up costs, a profit and loss forecast for the first year or two (or maybe three) and then a calculation of the break-even point. This is to show when the business expects to begin making a profit.

Then there is usually a People and Action Plan. This explains who is involved, and states their roles and responsibilities, their experience and abilities. The Action Plan explains what will happen in the important first year of the business, i.e. during the start-up phase.

Finally, the business plan has some information on the location, perhaps with photographs and architect's drawings. At the end there are the Appendices, containing any additional and detailed information or support material.

Gorliz & Zimmerman: Business Plan

April 6 2001

Contents

1.   Introduction: Business Outline

2.   M _ _ _ _ _ _ _ plan

2.1   P_ _ _ _ _ _ _ and s _ _ _ _ _ _ _

2.2   M _ _ _ _ _

2.3   P _ _ _ _ _ _ _ _ and s _ _ _ _ _ _

2.4   C _ _ _ _ _ _ _ _ _ _

3.   F _ _ _ _ _ _ _ _ plan

3.1   S _ _ _ _ – _ _ costs

3.2   P _ _ _ _ _ and l _ _ _ f _ _ _ _ _ _ _

3.3   B _ _ _ _ – e _ _ _ point

4. P _ _ _ _ _ and A _ _ _ _ _ plan

5. L _ _ _ _ _ _ _

6. A _ _ _ _ _ _ _ _ _

New businesses usually have a **business plan**. This is a document that describes what the new business is, how it will start up and how it will sell its goods and services. It also contains financial information.

There are different ways to structure a business plan. Some are shorter and simpler than the above model. Others are much more complicated.

41 Sequencing and timing: a Gantt chart

A key aspect of planning is sequencing and timing. A common management tool for this is the Gantt chart. Complete the missing words in the Actions using a word that means the same as the terms below (in the same order).

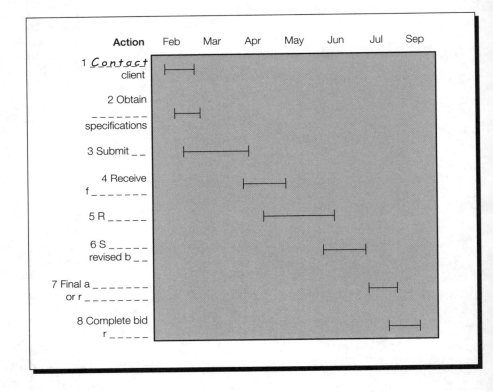

Action	Feb	Mar	Apr	May	Jun	Jul	Sep
1 *Contact* client							
2 Obtain _ _ _ _ _ _ specifications							
3 Submit _ _							
4 Receive f _ _ _ _ _ _							
5 R _ _ _ _ _							
6 S _ _ _ _ _ revised b _ _							
7 Final a _ _ _ _ _ _ _ or r _ _ _ _ _ _ _ _							
8 Complete bid r _ _ _ _ _							

1	speak to or write to	**5**	alter the (3)
2	written legal agreement	**6**	send (3) (to the client)
3	offer or tender	**7**	acceptance; non-acceptance
4	comments or suggestions	**8**	re-examination

 Henry L. Gantt (1861–1919) was an American management consultant.

42 Management By Objectives (MBO)

Management By Objectives (MBO) was originally developed by Peter Drucker (1985). Look at the diagram below and complete the dialogue underneath.

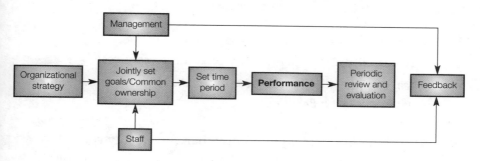

John: What is Management By Objectives?

Jane: MBO is a (1) _____*management*_____ approach. It is designed to help realize the (2) _____ of an organization.

John: The targets?

Jane: Yes.

John: So, how does MBO work?

Jane: The first thing is to have an organizational (3) _____. This is the method to reach the goals. But it is very important that (4) _____ and (5) _____ work together to create the goals.

John: So everyone owns the goals?

Jane: Exactly. Everyone's (6) _____ is vital. So the goals are agreed, as is the time period in which those goals should be achieved. Then the plan is put into action. This is (7) _____ . At this point, there is regular (8) _____ and (9) _____, a typical management task. But again, in MBO, everyone is involved. So everyone provides (10) _____.

- **Management By Objectives (MBO)** is about setting **targets** and measuring results against the targets.
- See also: Test 51 The control process

43 Total Quality Management (TQM)

TQM is a management philosophy in which quality is an absolute priority. Read the statements below. Fill in the spaces with a word that means the same as the word or phrase in italics below.

1 Product quality is the r e l i a b i l i t y, d _ _ _ _ _ _ _ _ _ , serviceability and dependability of goods or services.

extent to which the user can trust the product / extent to which the product will last a long time

2 TQM is a much wider philosophy than just quality control. TQM is a concept that covers the whole process of meeting c _ _ _ _ _ _ _ n _ _ _ _ .

what the buyer requires

3 TQM aims to ensure continual i _ _ _ _ _ _ _ _ _ in products and services.

better quality

4 TQM must be part of the overall c _ _ _ _ _ of the organization.

ethos and philosophy

5 TQM is essential to the s _ _ _ _ _ _ _ _ p _ _ _ _ _ _ of the organization.

long-term policy objectives

6 Successful TQM gives businesses a c _ _ _ _ _ _ _ _ _ a _ _ _ _ _ _ _ _ .

better prospects than other businesses in the same market

7 TQM uses s _ _ _ _ _ _ _ _ _ d _ _ _ to demonstrate improvements in quality.

numerical information from research

---

8 TQM includes customers and s _ _ _ _ _ _ _ _ in setting quality objectives.

companies who sell parts or components, or services, to other companies

---

9 TQM recommends improvement of employees' s _ _ _ _ _ through t _ _ _ _ _ _ _ .

abilities and competence / courses

---

10 TQM requires good p _ _ _ _ _ _ _ _ _ _ _ and c _ _ _ _ _ _ _ _ _ _ _ _ in t _ _ _ _ at all levels of the organization.

involvement / working together / groups

'I got laid off because I guess I made poor quality cars. In sixteen years not once was I ever asked how to do my job better. Not once.'
Redundant car worker (Drucker P., 1968, quoted in Hannagan, 1998, p.185).

Naturally, many 'management gurus' have written about the importance of quality. Peters and Waterman (1982) are two of the most important. See also Philip Crosby (1979) who emphasized the role of people responsible for quality improvement.

Here are two definitions of **Total Quality Management**:
'An intensive, long-term effort to transform all parts of an organization in order to produce the best product and service possible to meet customer needs' (Hannagan, 1998, p.174).

'An approach to control that integrates quality objectives into all management functions to continually achieve higher quality'
(Black and Porter, 2000, p.498).

44 Corporate strategy

Corporate strategy is described below as a combination of eight aspects.
Read the questions on the left and choose the correct answer from the box.

action plan	analysis of resources	audit of external
corporate objectives	environment	marketing plan
market research	~~mission statement~~	strategic plan

1	What is our business?	*mission statement*
2	Where do we want to go?	_____
3	Who are our customers? What do they need?	_____
4	What threats and opportunities are there?	_____
5	What are our strengths and weaknesses?	_____
6	How do we achieve our goals in terms of marketing?	_____
7	How do we get to where we want to be, with our present resources?	_____
8	What do we have to do now?	_____

The **corporate strategy** of an organization combines:

• a statement of the core functions of the business

• its aims and goals

• how to achieve its aims and goals

Corporate strategy is both an overview of where the organization is now and a description of what is necessary to take it forward.

45 Strategic management

Strategic management is how a business tries to achieve its goals, using any available resources. The Billy Goats Gruff is a Norwegian fairystory about three goats who fight for their freedom against a monster – and win.

Big Billy Goat Gruff: *'We are here and we want to go there. We need a strategic plan.'*

– First ... then ... then ... finally ...

– I'm going to eat you up.
– No! My brother is coming soon and he's bigger than me.
– Okay! You can go!

– I'm going to eat you up.
– No! My brother is coming soon and he's bigger than me.
– Okay! You can go!

– I'm going to eat you up.
– Oh, no you're not!

– Aaagh!
– Success!

Mark the following statements True or False.

1	Strategic management is a process, not a single event.	(True)/False
2	Strategic management involves top managers and not subordinates.	True/False
3	Good strategic management monitors results and makes changes.	True/False
4	Strategic management is concerned with actual resources, not future resources.	True/False
5	Strategic management uses tools like the 'product life cycle' to plan future actions.	True/False
6	Bill Gates is a good example of an effective strategic manager.	True/False
7	Strategic management is the same as having a strategic plan.	True/False
8	Corporate strategy and strategic management are the same thing.	True/False

46 Portfolio analysis

Portfolio analysis was originally created by the Boston Consulting Group (BCG). It uses the Boston Matrix, a management tool to help companies make maximum profit from their complete range of products or services.

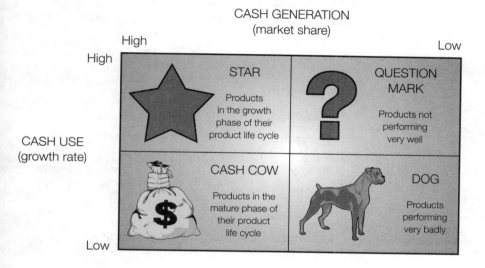

Mark the following statements as True or False.

1	The Boston Matrix is a strategic planning tool.	(True)/False
2	Managers can compare the finances of Strategic Business Units (SBUs) inside one company.	True/False
3	An SBU is a cash cow.	True/False
4	Dogs often become stars and make a lot of money.	True/False
5	Cash cows require a lot of investment.	True/False
6	Stars have low market share but a lot of potential.	True/False
7	Question marks may become dogs or stars.	True/False
8	Cash cows may become dogs.	True/False
9	The Boeing 747 is the cash cow of the Boeing Corporation.	True/False
10	An example of cash cows that became dogs is the 5.25" floppy disk.	True/False

47 Management organization

A Management of a large company is often hierarchical. Here is a typical model of management organization showing one division within a company. Complete any missing words. If you have problems, look at the box below.

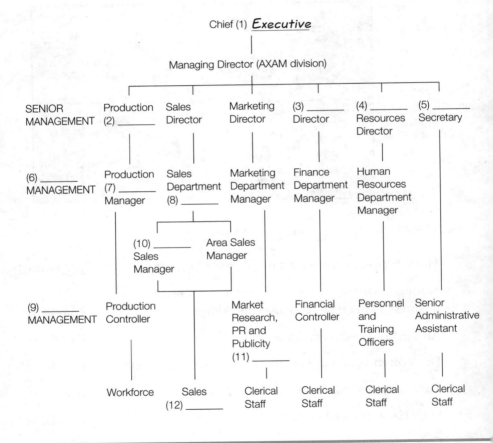

Chief (1) *Executive*
|
Managing Director (AXAM division)

SENIOR MANAGEMENT	Production (2) _____	Sales Director	Marketing Director	(3) _____ Director	(4) _____ Resources Director	(5) _____ Secretary

(6) _____ MANAGEMENT	Production (7) _____ Manager	Sales Department (8) _____	Marketing Department Manager	Finance Department Manager	Human Resources Department Manager

(10) _____ Sales Manager   Area Sales Manager

(9) _____ MANAGEMENT	Production Controller	Market Research, PR and Publicity (11) _____	Financial Controller	Personnel and Training Officers	Senior Administrative Assistant

	Workforce	Sales (12) _____	Clerical Staff	Clerical Staff	Clerical Staff	Clerical Staff

Area	Company	Department	Director	~~Executive~~	Finance
	Human	Junior	Manager	Middle	Officers	Teams

B   Choose the correct words in italics.

1   The organization model opposite is a *flat/hierarchical* structure.

2   The model shows *a traditional structure/an innovative structure*.

3   The model shows a *matrix/functional* structure.

4   It is probably a *services/manufacturing* company.

5   It is typical of a *small or medium-sized enterprise (SME)/large enterprise*.

6   The business is probably *simple/complex*.

A **matrix structure** is a management structure that is in part based on hierarchy but also based on **project management**, so special **teams** are created for specific tasks. In these project teams the structure is often much less hierarchical. A matrix structure involves teams with varying membership. A matrix structure is most common in **small or medium-sized organizations (SMEs)**.

48 Information and data handling

A Information helps managers reduce risk in decision-making. In the computer-age, information systems have been revolutionized. Match words on the left with words on the right to make phrases.

1	information	interchange
2	data	user
3	artificial	technology
4	electronic funds	processing
5	electronic data	intelligence
6	information system	transfer
7	end	security

B Complete the crossword. All the terms are used in data handling.

Across

1 Computers help users to exchange _____. (11)

4 Passwords protect _____. (8)

7 _____ changes fast. (10)

8 Another word for transfer. (11)

10 Financial resources or money. (5)

11 A person working at a computer terminal is an end _____. (4)

12 Using a computer to work with facts and figures: data _____. (10)

Down

2 Robots use an artificial form of this. (12)

3 Computers make use of _____ intelligence. (10)

5 _____ devices contain microchips. (10)

6 A computer _____ consists of hardware and software. (6)

9 Moving data from computer to computer. (8)

 The word *data* is usually used in singular form, i.e. *the data is ...* rather than *the data are...* The word *information* is uncountable and is therefore used with a singular verb, i.e. *the information is ...*

49 Operations management

'Operations management is a specialized field of management associated with the conversion or transformation of resources into products and services.'

(Black and Porter, 2000)

Choose the correct explanation a) or b) for each of the aspects of operations management (1–15).

1	Logistics	(a) Another term for operations management.
		b) Computer studies of design systems.

2	Facility layout	a) Organization of departments.
		b) Position of things and people in a work space or factory.

3	Facility location	a) Geographical position of a work place.
		b) Place where the staff eat and relax.

4	Production line layout	a) Organization of staff in a factory.
		b) Position of machinery and people in a factory.

5	Capacity planning	a) Process of deciding how much a work place should produce.
		b) Deciding when to operate at 100% production level.

6	Design capacity	a) Ideal production level.
		b) Maximum possible level of output.

7	Effective capacity	a) The percentage of design capacity a facility should operate at.
		b) The percentage of capacity required to make a profit.

8	Materials requirement planning (MRP)	a) Purchasing materials in the planning stage of a project.
		b) Computer system to work out what is needed from suppliers, how much is needed and when.

9	Productivity	a) Measurement of output in relation to investment (input).
		b) Total volume of production in one year.

10	Flowchart	a) Process designed to improve quality control.
		b) Diagram showing the stages in a process.

11	Bench-marking	a) System of calculating the number of staff required for a project.
		b) Using the high standards of competitor organizations as a comparison to improve quality.

12	Just-in-time systems	a) Way to improve punctuality among workers by paying them more.
		b) Control system to ensure that materials are received and deliveries made at exactly the right moment to eliminate storage and waste in production processes.

13	Computer-integrated manufacturing (CIM)	a) Integration of information systems and equipment in manufacturing to ensure quality products.
		b) Using computers to design world-class products.

14	Computer-aided design (CAD)	a) Computer software to assist in designing products, making small changes and product testing.
		b) Computer design centre for advertising new high-tech products.

15	Flexible manufacturing system (FMS)	a) Total automation of a production facility by controlling everything with a computer.
		b) Matching orders to production.

50 Human Resources

A The words below relate to the functions of human resource management. Complete the spaces in the table.

NOUN: THING	NOUN: PERSON	VERB
analysis	analyst	_____
_____	appraiser/ _appraisee_	appraise
compensation	_____	_____
_____	developer	_____
_____	_____/employee	employ
_____	interviewer/_____	_____
_____	recruiter	_____
_____	trainer/_____	_____
plan	_____	_____
selection	selector	_____

B Complete each two-word phrase in the sentences below with an appropriate word from the box.

> appraisal   career   ceiling   harassment   ~~in-service~~
> opportunities   redundancies   retirement   reward   rotation
> sharing   simulation   structured   vacant

1 Training given to employees, often by an external provider, is called ____in-service____ training.

2 An interview process where interviewers ask set questions in a fixed order is called a _____ interview.

3 If two people agree to work part time on the same job, dividing the job between them, this is called job- _____.

4 An interview or training situation which uses a model of a real situation is called a work _____.

5 An interview, usually carried out at regular intervals of perhaps six or twelve months, to discuss an employee's career progress and achievement of certain targets, is called a performance

_____.

6 Where a particular post in an organization is held for a set period – for example a year – by one person and then given to another person, this is called job _____.

7 Different ways of paying or compensating employees for their work and performance are called _____ systems.

8 Unwanted attention in the workplace of a sexual nature, often verbal, physical or psychological, is called sexual

_____.

9 A policy of ensuring that all employees or prospective employees, e.g. job applicants, are treated fairly, without any regard to gender, race, colour, religion, sexual orientation, age or beliefs, is called an equal _____ policy.

10 A possible plan showing an individual's job development or changing responsibilities in a company over time is called a _____ path.

11 The tendency for women to rise to a certain level in a company hierarchy – and then to find that further promotion is blocked by male prejudice or tradition (often the same thing) – is sometimes described as encountering a glass _____.

12 Pages in newspapers, magazines or on websites offering employment possibilities are called situations _____ columns.

13 Stopping work before the usual age for a pension is called taking early _____.

14 If a company dismisses workers who do not want to lose their jobs, this is called making compulsory _____.

51 The control process

Complete the dialogue below with suitable words from the box.

action	alterations	communication	constant	feedback
flowchart	goals	goal-setting	measure	monitoring
objectives	outcomes	performance	~~process~~	setting

Student: So, we've looked at different areas of management control. How actually does a manager carry out the control function in his or her job?

Trainer: Good question! Well, control is a (1) ___*process*___ .

Student: Of course.

Trainer: Management is dynamic, change is a constant. So control is also a (2) _____. Management control is a process of (3) _____ and (4) _____ organizational activities to meet organizational (5) _____. This process involves constant (6) _____ at all levels, so (7) _____ is very important.

Student: Is it possible to construct a (8) _____ to illustrate the process?

Trainer: Yes, I think we can. First we have the desired (9) _____. These are part of agreed (10) _____. The manager then establishes (11) _____ plans, and ways to monitor (12) _____.

Student: And so we (13) _____ performance.

Trainer: Correct. And the next step?

Student: We compare performance with targets and make any necessary (14) _____. We may also change aspects of the work.

Trainer: Yes. We can complete a loop here, through feedback. This informs future action and (15) _____.

THE CONTROL PROCESS

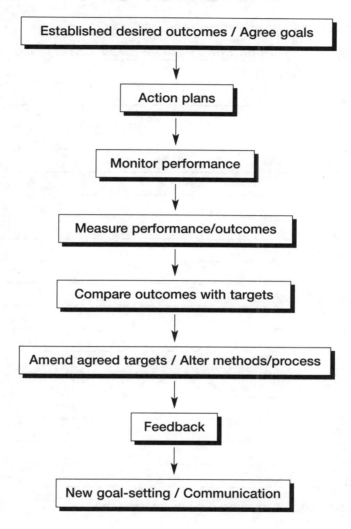

Established desired outcomes / Agree goals

↓

Action plans

↓

Monitor performance

↓

Measure performance/outcomes

↓

Compare outcomes with targets

↓

Amend agreed targets / Alter methods/process

↓

Feedback

↓

New goal-setting / Communication

See also: Test 42 Management By Objectives

52 Management abbreviations

A What do the following abbreviations stand for?

1 SME _Small and Medium-sized Enterprises_

2 BCG _____

3 MBO _____

4 MBWA _____

5 TQM _____

6 QUEST _____

7 ROI _____

8 SBU _____

9 SWOT _____

10 CAD _____

11 CAM _____

12 DSS _____

13 HR _____

14 IT _____

15 JIT _____

16 MRP _____

17 FMS _____

18 BEP _____

19 CEO _____

20 OB _____

B Decide which of the above is concerned with:

1 The culture and practices within a company or organization. _OB_

2 The volume of production required before there is any profit. _____

3 The boss in a large company or organization. _____

4 Total automation of a production process. _____

5 Working out what is required, and when, from suppliers. _____

6 Ensuring there is no waste through storage of components or finished products. _____

7 Everything to do with personnel. _____

8 A motif for ensuring quality in everything the company does. _____

9 A management approach based on goal-setting, monitoring results and making necessary changes. _____

10 A specialist firm that created a tool to help analyse the success of individual products and product areas. _____

11 Everything to do with hardware and software. _____

12 Businesses employing fewer than 200 people. _____

13 A method of analysing the profitability of a company or activity. _____

14 An individual cost centre in terms of its contribution to the wider company activities, perhaps based around one product or group of related products. _____

15 A combination of tools, both in software and in other forms, to help managers in decision-making. _____

16 A key management function described by Peters and Waterman (1982) which involves going around and looking, listening and thinking about what is going on. _____

17 A tool for planning marketing that involves examining factors inside and outside the business or organization. _____

18 Computer software used in manufacturing industries to help product design. _____

19 Computer software to help with operations management in manufacturing. _____

20 A management approach based on quality in all aspects of company activity from sourcing, dealing with suppliers, treatment of employees, relations with customers, product design, manufacture and delivery, after-sales service and relations with the community. _____

Notice the pronunciation of the names of the following letters (vowels):
- A /eɪ/ as in *pay*
- E /iː/ as in *me*
- I /aɪ/ as in *my*
- O /əʊ/ as in *owe*
- U /juː/ as in *you*

53 Financial control

NEW 5000-ROOM HOTEL OPENS

Company Chairman Fred Hopeful says:

'With the current high currency valuation, the decline in tourism and rocketing oil prices, and the general economic decline, we expect to break even by about 2093.'

Financial control depends on doing the right thing at the right time. Financial control also depends on analysis of various key indicators. Match the words in the box to the correct definition (1–7).

| break-even point | budgetary control | efficiency | leverage |
| liquidity | ~~profitability~~ | return on investment (ROI) |

1 Ratio of cost to benefit. _____*profitability*_____

2 Total income ÷ total investment = measure of profitability.

3 Measure of how well a business can meet its short-term cash needs.

4 Ratio of total debt to total assets.

5 Ratio of amount of sales to total cost.

6 Volume of sales needed to cover costs and begin to produce profit.

7 System to ensure that financial targets are met.

Notice the following word families.

noun	adjective	verb
liquid, liquidity	liquid	to liquefy
efficiency	efficient	—
profit, profitability	profitable	to profit (from something)

54 Research and Development (R&D)

It is very important to carry out research before entering a new market, or developing new products. Choose the correct definitions for each term. In some cases, more than one definition is correct.

1	Marketing research	a)	Studies to find information that will inform marketing policy.
		b)	Studies of consumers and customers.
		c)	Research to find out where to sell products.

2	Research	a)	Studies to find out what a company should do.
		b)	The same as Research and Development.
		c)	A report on research.

3	Development	a)	Increased sales for a product.
		b)	Selling into export markets.
		c)	Work on creating a product for a target market.

4	Primary research	a)	The first research a company does on a particular problem.
		b)	Original research carried out by a company.
		c)	Information sold by specialist agencies.

5	Desk research	a)	Research which is based on published material, internet, etc.
		b)	Studies into the cost of office equipment.
		c)	Study of a new market or location without actually visiting.

6	Secondary research	a)	Research that is out of date.
		b)	Studies which are available to the public from government or specialist agencies, perhaps free, perhaps at a cost.
		c)	Poor-quality research.

7	Field research	a)	This is also known as fieldwork.
		b)	Physical activity of visiting a location to find out information through person-to-person interviews.
		c)	Reading published material.

8	Market research	a)	Studies to find out about consumers.
		b)	Studies to find out strengths and weaknesses of products.
		c)	Studies to find out what consumers think of different companies.

Development is not the same as research, although the terms are often used together in the phrase **research and development (R&D)**. Research takes place before a product is made and launched. In this phase research coincides with development. Later, further research may indicate changes to an established successful product. In this case, the product may be developed over many years, with innovations to keep up to date with technical improvements and changing customer needs.

55 International organizations

A What do these abbreviations stand for?

1 NAFTA _North American Free Trade Agreement_

2 OPEC _____

3 EU _____

4 NATO _____

5 UN _____

6 WTO _____

7 WHO _____

8 ASEAN _____

9 IMF _____

10 ECB _____

11 FDA _____

12 OECD _____

13 MNCs _____

14 FIFA _____

B The companies below are all MNCs (multinational corporations). What do their initials stand for?

1 GM _General Motors_

2 IBM _____

3 CNN _____

4 NEC _____

5 JAL _____

56 International marketing

Companies which want to expand into international markets need to consider many factors. Match each of the factors (1–12) to an appropriate explanation (a–l).

Factors for consideration   **Meaning**

1 Location and distance

2 Political context

3 Labour costs

4 Infrastructure

5 Distribution channels

6 Labour factors

7 Economic environment

8 Business culture

9 National culture

10 Legislative environment

11 Socio-cultural factors

12 Fixed costs

a Skills, training and flexibility of workforce.

b Transportation, roads, telecommunications, public services.

c Investment needed for land, property, energy (light, heating, fuel).

d Typical business practices, security, commercial expectations.

e Way of life, public and private differences in language, religion, values and expectations.

f Cost of living, inflation, interest rates, taxes, growth, financial stability.

g Stability, system of government, democracy, human rights.

h Salaries and wages for local staff.

i Geographical position in relation to home base.

j Birth rate, life expectancy, literacy, average level of education.

k Systems for selling goods and services.

l Laws, trade regulations, membership of international groups.

- Companies enter international markets to increase their turnover and profits. Large **multinational companies** from developed countries may locate operations in developing countries because labour is cheaper. They may also set up in other developed countries because they want to be closer to new markets and to reduce **distribution costs**.
- See also: Test 6 Marketing

57 Working across frontiers

A A business that wants to set up an operation in another country has to do a lot of research and planning. Read the e-mail below from someone who is planning to set up an office to sell products in a new market. Complete the gaps (1–32) in the e-mail with suitable words.

B There are five sections in the e-mail below. Label each section (1–5) with one of the terms in the box.

Bureaucracy   ~~Culture~~   Financial issues   Marketing   Property

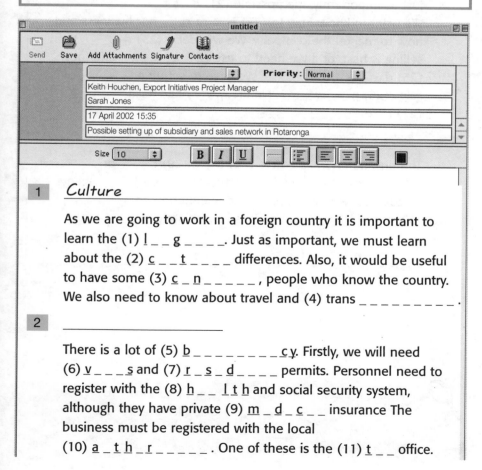

Size 10

1 _Culture_

As we are going to work in a foreign country it is important to learn the (1) l _ _ g _ _ _ _. Just as important, we must learn about the (2) c _ _ t _ _ _ _ differences. Also, it would be useful to have some (3) c _ n _ _ _ _ _ _, people who know the country. We also need to know about travel and (4) trans _ _ _ _ _ _ _ _.

2 _____

There is a lot of (5) b _ _ _ _ _ _ _ _ c y. Firstly, we will need (6) v _ _ _ s and (7) r _ s _ d _ _ _ _ permits. Personnel need to register with the (8) h _ _ l t h and social security system, although they have private (9) m _ d _ c _ _ insurance The business must be registered with the local (10) a _ t h _ r _ _ _ _ _. One of these is the (11) t _ _ office.

3 _____

Research is necessary on possible government (12) g _ _ n t s to new businesses. There might be (13) t _ _ incentives for setting up new activities. We must learn about the (14) l _ g _ l framework. There might be import or export (15) d _ t _ _ _ _ . Our business also needs local (16) b _ _ k _ _ _ facilities, bank (17) a _ c _ _ n _ _ and foreign (18) c _ r r _ _ _ _ services.

4 _____

A lot of (19) m a r _ _ _   r _ _ _ _ _ _ _ is required.
We have to know about the (20) c _ m p _ _ _ _ _ _ n , and just as importantly, the possible (21) c _ s t _ _ _ _ _ .
We want to know how to (22) p _ _ m o _ _ our business and how to market the company. We wonder if (23) d _ _ _ _ t selling is best, or if we need to use (24) a _ e _ t _ and local (25) d _ _ t r _ b _ _ _ _ _ . We have to set up a sales (26) n _ _ w _ _ _ . Naturally, we need local (27) r _ p r e _ _ _ _ _ _ _ _ _ _ .

5 _____

The question here is do we (28) b _ _ , (29) r _ _ _ or (30) l _ _ s e? We should contact local (31) e s t _ _ _ agents. Of course the business will need telephone and (32) c _ _ _ _ _ _ r connections immediately.

The word *research* is only used in the singular. Note the verb phrases:
to do research, to carry out research, to undertake research
and the noun or noun phrases:
research, research costs, research and development (R&D).

58 Globalization

> A definition of globalization:
>
> 'A condition marked by decreasing geographical constraints affecting *trade, communication, security, aid, investment, industrial and commercial ownership, wealth generation* and *environmental awareness.*'

Which words from the definition above do you associate with each of the factors below?

1 multinational corporations *trade, industrial and commercial ownership, investment, wealth generation*

2 Internet _____

3 air transportation _____

4 defence and military alliances _____

5 loans to developing countries _____

6 global warming _____

7 transnational companies _____

8 WTO _____

9 NATO _____

10 NAFTA _____

11 UN _____

12 tourism _____

13 information technology _____

14 share ownership _____

15 global capitalism _____

16 franchise operations _____

17 AIDS _____

18 population growth _____

19 Microsoft _____

20 US Supreme Court _____

Globalization reaches the remotest parts.

  The fact that the 20 terms in the list are related to so many aspects of globalization is an indication of how important globalization has become in our lives.

59 Cultural issues

A Below are sixteen different cultural values. Match 1–8 to the contrasting phrase in a–h.

1	individualist culture	a	egalitarian culture
2	consensus-minded culture	b	high-context culture
3	deferential culture	c	specialist and technocratic management
4	high job-mobility	d	soft, customer-focused
5	low-context culture	e	low job-mobility
6	loyalty to the company	f	group-oriented culture
7	broad-based managerial skills	g	loyalty to oneself
8	hard, corporate values	h	competitive culture

B Complete the sentences below with a phrase from part A.

1 A culture where people work collaboratively and co-operatively and do not try to stand out from the group, and where community interests are much more important than personal ambition is a ___*group-oriented culture*___.

2 A culture where managers pay a great deal of respect to their seniors or their elders, and where subordinates show respect and humility towards managers, is a _____.

3 A culture where typically people stay in the same job for many years, probably living near their family home, has

_____.

4 In a culture where managers typically have a wide range of abilities and are not necessarily specialists, it is important to have

_____.

5 A corporate culture where there is the view that the company exists to serve customers, and that the customer is king, can be described as _____.

6 A culture where little attention is paid to relationship-building, where business is the priority, is a _____.

7 Where employees represent and defend their company, and respect and identify with its values, there is strong

_____.

8 A culture where everyone is trying to increase a range of personal benefits, including their own status and identity within the group, is a _____.

'Come on! This company has a 'competitive, go-getting can-do culture'!'

See also: Test 21 Cultural variance

60 Global issues and the future

This test is the result of a brainstorm on developments in the next fifty years. Match each of the predictions (1–11) with evidence for it (a–k).

1 Less use of oil as main source of energy.

a The US dollar takes over completely under the World Bank.

2 More leisure time.

b A stronger and fairer World Trade Organization.

3 Breakup of multinational companies.

c More use of solar power.

4 Revolution in house design.

d More use of gene therapy and less disease.

5 A world currency.

e An end to the gap in wealth between rich and poor countries.

6 Frequent space travel.

f People working fewer hours.

7 More genuine free trade around the world.

g Fewer global companies, more small and regional businesses.

8 More respect for the environment.

h Solar-powered capsules on monorails.

9 New transportation methods.

i Holidays on the moon.

10 A fairer world.

j New kinds of domestic architecture.

11 Massive advances in medical science.

k An end to waste in production and consumption.

Answers

Test 1

1 e	2 g	3 a	4 j	5 b
6 c	7 h	8 d	9 k	10 f
11 l	12 i			

Test 2

PLANNING	ORGANIZING
identifying needs	putting systems
setting objectives	in place
deciding strategy	*managing resources*
identifying change	time management
taking on new staff	
LEADING	**CONTROLLING**
communicating with	*comparing results*
staff	*with targets*
team-building	monitoring quality
supervision	standards
motivation	
empowering staff	
to take decisions	

Test 3

1 Managers are responsible for 'the **process** of **planning**, **organizing**, **leading** and **controlling** the efforts of **organization** members and of using all organizational **resources** to achieve stated organizational **goals**'.

3 '(Management is) the process of optimizing **human**, **material** and **financial** contributions for the achievement of organizational goals'.

4 A modern view of management, expressed by Sir Roland Smith, is that 'Management should be based on **innovation**, **marketing** and risk'.

5 'All managers may be involved with the operational aspects of management but as they are promoted and develop, their role becomes increasingly one of **planning**, **innovation** and **leadership**'.

6 Management is 'the **process** of **assembling** and using resources – **human**, **financial** and **material**, and **information** – in a goal-directed manner to accomplish tasks in an **organization**'.

Test 4

1 emotionally strong
2 mental skills
3 good communicator
4 technically skilled
5 flexible
6 social skills
7 creative
8 leadership
9 sensitive to others
10 knowledgeable

Test 5

1 a	2 b	3 a	4 b
5 a	6 a	7 a	8 b

Test 6

A 1 Selling <u>things</u> that don't come back to <u>people</u> who do.
2 <u>Everything</u> a company does to influence <u>demand</u> for its products and services.
3 <u>Promoting</u> and selling goods and <u>services</u>.

B 1 Product
2 Price
3 Place
4 Promotion
5 People
6 Process
7 Physical evidence

Test 7

1 False		4 True
2 False		5 True
3 True		6 False

Test 8
1 Just-In-Time
2 Corporate downsizing
3 Empowerment
4 Teamworking
5 Re-engineering
6 Total Quality Management
7 Outsourcing
8 Learning organizations

Test 9
A
1 True 5 True
2 True 6 False
3 False 7 False
4 False 8 True

B

Theory X	Theory Y
work is a necessity	communication
direction	participation
traditional	co-operation
orders	creativity
control	modern
security	work is natural

Test 10
Autocratic leadership
directive ✓ hierarchical ✓ traditional ✓

Democratic leadership
group-oriented ✓ team-based ✓
communicative ✓

Laissez-faire leadership
open ✓ co-operative ✓ creative ✓

Charismatic
personality-driven ✓ goal-oriented ✓
inspirational ✓

Test 11
1 innovators 4 monitors
2 producers 5 controller
3 mentors 6 leader

Test 12
A
1 b
2 d
3 a
4 e
5 c

Test 13
A
1 drives 4 behaves
2 reach 5 willingness
3 outcomes 6 effort
B Level 1 Physiological needs
Level 2 Safety needs
Level 3 Social needs
Level 4 Esteem needs
Level 5 Self-actualization

Test 14
1 win 5 concessions
2 common 6 Fighter
3 agreement 7 Creative
4 demands 8 Win/lose

Test 15
A
1 objectives
2 definitions
3 leader, teams
4 costs, budget
5 tender
6 proposals
7 negotiate
8 contracts
9 plan, schedule
10 support
11 monitor
12 results
B
1 objectives / l aims
2 definitions / b terms
3 leader / d co-ordinator
teams / i groups
4 costs / n expenses
budget / o financial plan
5 tender / f offers
6 proposals / g submissions
7 negotiate / a discuss
8 contracts / j agreements
9 plan /c organize
schedule / e set time targets
10 support / k assistance
11 monitor / h check
12 results / m outcomes

Test 16

1 B w	3 A z	5 D v
2 E x	4 C y	

Test 17

A
1. Values (C)
2. Having a clear structure (O)
3. Beliefs (C)
4. Formal sources of authority (O)
5. Assumptions and attitudes (C)
6. Norms (C)
7. Objectives/Common purpose (C)
8. Relationship between centre/periphery (O)
9. Shared experience (C)
10. The system (O)

B A: How is organizational **culture** created? What is it?
B: Organizational culture is a set of basic **assumptions** or what people think, in a company or organization.
A: So it's based on common **values**?
B: That's right. Everyone learns these over time They learn the way of doing things, the **norms**.
A: And everyone agrees that they are right?
B: Generally, yes.
A: And where do they come from?
B: From shared experience. From history, tradition and common **beliefs**.
A: And new employees usually learn the same things? They learn the **system**.
B: Exactly. Everyone learns the same organizational culture.

Test 18

1. traditional
2. flat
3. closed
4. informal
5. rules, regulations
6. market
7. top-down
8. flexible, departments
9. Creativity
10. systems, people

Test 19

R	I	M	K	**S**	**Y**	**M**	**B**	**O**	**L**	**S**
C	A	**L**	**A**	**N**	**G**	**U**	**A**	**G**	**E**	N
C	**E**	**R**	**E**	**M**	**O**	**N**	**I**	**E**	**S**	I
Z	A	H	N	Y	E	I	R	O	T	L
U	Y	E	O	T	Q	F	X	P	O	N
L	J	R	C	H	T	O	C	E	R	N
S	**P**	**O**	**N**	**S**	**O**	**R**	**S**	**H**	**I**	**P**
Z	A	E	P	D	K	M	F	G	E	W
H	I	S	L	N	S	S	T	T	S	U
M	**A**	**G**	**A**	**Z**	**I**	**N**	**E**	F	C	M
V	R	E	M	R	**A**	**W**	**A**	**R**	**D**	**S**

1. uniforms
2. language
3. magazine
4. sponsorship
5. heroes
6. awards, ceremonies
7. stories, myths
8. symbols

Test 20

1. dimensions
2. power distance
3. subordinates
4. uncertainty avoidance
5. threat
6. Individualism
7. collective
8. masculinity
9. femininity
10. Assertiveness
11. competitiveness
12. masculine
13. environment

Test 21

1 c	2 i	3 h	4 d	5 e
6 j	7 g	8 a	9 f	10 b

Test 22

A
1. e
2. a
3. b
4. f
5. c
6. d

B 1 organizational
2 groups
3 influence/ status/ control
4 control/ influence
5 lose
6 looking
7 compromise
8 status / influence

Test 23

1	g	5	f (or possibly h)
2	c	6	h (or possibly f)
3	i	7	b
4	e	8	a
		9	d

Test 24

1 (h) Competition factors
2 (a) International environment
3 (f) Domestic environment
4 (g) Government/legal factors
5 (b) Technological environment
6 (e) Environmental pressures
7 (c) Consumer needs/wants
8 (d) Industry environment

Test 25

A

1	False	5	True
2	False	6	False
3	True	7	True
4	True		

B Higher profits
• **Quality**-based competition
• Few competitors
• Difficult **market** to enter
• Few new players in the market
• Few substitutes
• Many **customers**
• Many suppliers
• **Fragmented** customers
Lower profits
• Price-based competition
• Many **competitors**
• Easy market to enter
• Many new players in the market
• Many **substitutes**
• Few customers
• Few **suppliers**
• United customers

Test 26

1 g H
2 f E
3 d I
4 h C
5 j D
6 i F
7 c J
8 b A
9 e B
10 a G

Test 27

	A		**B**	
1	A	L, E	B	child labour
2	A	L, ENV	B	air pollution
3	A	L, E	B	working conditions
4	A	L	B	fraud
5	A	CC, L	B	food standards
6	A	CC	B	reliability
7	A	ENV, L	B	soil contamination
8	A	CC, L	B	safety standards

Test 28

1 **A** product testing
B CP
2 **A** safety mask for a welder
B H&S
3 **A** safety cap on a cleaning agent
B CP
4 **A** ergonomics
B H&S
5 **A** vivisection
B CP
6 **A** air-conditioning
B H&S
7 **A** warning notice on a paint tin
B CP/H&S
8 **A** protective clothing
B H&S

Test 29

1 advertising
2 impulse
3 testing
4 vivisection
5 whistle
6 opportunities
7 confidential
8 gifts
9 hospitality
10 promotion

Test 30

1 c	2 e	3 a	4 b	5 g
6 d	7 i	8 j	9 f	10 h

Test 31

1 j	2 f	3 a	4 d	5 g
6 h	7 b	8 e	9 i	10 c

Test 32

1 predict
2 assess
3 set
4 plan
5 implement
6 monitor
7 measure
8 reward

Test 33

1 innovation
2 invention
3 inventor
4 patent
5 development
6 market
7 diffusion
8 range
9 integration
10 decline

Test 34

1 training manager
2 retraining
3 qualification
4 graduate
5 curriculum vitae (CV)
6 research
7 skills audit
8 training budget
9 human resources
10 seminar
11 staff development
12 lecture
13 trainer
14 trainee
15 in-service training

Test 35

1 b	2 h	3 g	4 f
5 c	6 e	7 d	8 a

Test 36

A
1 discussion
2 teleconferencing
3 quality circles
4 voice-mail
5 internal mail/memos
6 post
7 intranet
8 extranet

B **Written/printed communication**
memos
notice-board
company reports
newsletters
post
internal mail

Speech communication
face-to-face
departmental meeting
formal presentations
quality circles

Machine communication
e-mail
fax
internet
voice-mail
intranet
telephone
extranet
video-tape
teleconferencing

Test 37

Stage I
Planning and preparation

Stage II
Relationship building between negotiating parties

Stage III
Information exchange

Stage IV
Persuasion attempts

Stage V
Concessions or compromise and agreement

Test 38

1 strategic plan
2 planning
3 objectives
4 tactical plan
5 operational plan
6 interim plan
7 provisional plan
8 business plan
9 action plan
10 budget
11 contingency plan

Test 41

1 **Contact** client
2 Obtain **contract** specifications
3 Submit **bid**
4 Receive **feedback**
5 **Revise bid**
6 **Submit** revised bid
7 Final **approval** or **rejection**
8 Complete bid **review**

Test 39

Expo Marketing Consultants	
SWOT Analysis for GUBU (Toys) Ltd	
Strengths 1 Reliable and committed workforce 2 Use of wood – seen as 'good for the environment' 5 Beautiful handmade toys	**Weaknesses** 3 High labour costs 4 Location – far from population centres / far from new markets 6 Poor communications systems / limited technological skills 8 Lack of IT training in staff
Opportunities 7 Internet as potential marketing tool / e-commerce 10 Potentially strong demand in Germany and Scandinavia 13 Selling by new channels, e.g. mail order	**Threats** 9 Declining interest in domestic markets for traditional toys 11 Competition in Germany and Scandinavia / Baltic countries 12 Increased competition from mail order companies

Test 40

2 **Marketing** plan
  2.1 **Products** and **services**
  2.2 **Promotion** and **selling**
  2.3 **Market**
  2.4 **Competition**
3 **Financial** plan
  3.1 **Start-up** costs
  3.2 **Profit** and **loss forecast**
  3.3 **Break-even** point
4 **People** and **Action** plan
5 **Location**
6 **Appendices**

Test 42

1 management
2 goals
3 strategy
4 management
5 staff
6 Ownership
7 performance
8 review
9 evaluation
10 feedback

Test 43

1 reliability, durability
2 customer needs
3 improvement
4 culture
5 strategic planning
6 competitive advantage
7 statistical data
8 suppliers
9 skills, training
10 participation, collaboration, teams

Test 44

1 mission statement
2 corporate objectives
3 market research
4 audit of external environment
5 analysis of resources
6 marketing plan
7 strategic plan
8 action plan

Test 45

1 True
2 False. Normally strategic management involves a lot of communication and feedback, so subordinates have an important role. However, top management have the main responsibility.
3 True
4 False. Future needs are also considered, so new resources may be obtained from investment.
5 True
6 True
7 False. The strategic plan is part of strategic management.
8 False. Strategic management is a necessary process in order to achieve the objectives of the corporate strategy.

Test 46

1 True
2 False. It may be, but not necessarily.
3 True
4 False. They lose money and usually die.
5 False. They generate a lot of income for relatively low investment.
6 False. Stars have high market share and high potential.
7 True
8 True
9 True
10 True

Test 47

A 1 Executive
   2 Director
   3 Finance
   4 Human
   5 Company
   6 Middle
   7 Department
   8 Manager
   9 Junior
   10 Area
   11 Officers
   12 Teams
B 1 hierarchical
   2 traditional structure
   3 functional
   4 manufacturing
   5 large enterprise
   6 complex

Test 48

A 1 information technology
   2 data processing
   3 artificial intelligence
   4 electronic funds transfer
   5 electronic data interchange
   6 information system security
   7 end user

Test 48
B

Crossword grid:

	¹I	N	F	O	R	M	A	T	²I	O	N	
									N			
³A			⁴S	⁵E	C	U	R	I	T	Y		
R				L				E				⁶S
T			⁷T	E	C	H	N	O	L	O	G	Y
I				C				L				S
F				T				I				T
⁸I	N	⁹T	E	R	C	H	A	N	G	E		E
C		R		O				E				M
I		A		N			¹⁰F	U	N	D	S	
A		N		I				C				
L		S		C			¹¹U	S	E	R		
		F										
		E										
¹²P	R	O	C	E	S	S	I	N	G			

Test 49

1 a	2 b	3 a	4 b	5 a
6 b	7 a	8 b	9 a	10 b
11 b	12 b	13 a	14 a	15 a

Test 50

A NOUN: THING
analysis, appraisal, compensation, development, employment, interview, plan, recruitment, selection, training

NOUN: PERSON
analyst, appraiser/appraisee none, developer, employer/ employee, interviewer/ interviewee, planner, recruiter selector, trainer/trainee

VERB
analyse, appraise, compensate, develop, employ, interview, plan, recruit, select, train

B
1 in-service training
2 structured interview
3 job-sharing
4 work simulation
5 performance appraisal
6 job rotation
7 reward systems
8 sexual harassment
9 equal opportunities
10 career path
11 glass ceiling
12 situations vacant
13 early retirement
14 compulsory redundancies

Test 51
1 process
2 constant
3 setting
4 monitoring
5 objectives / goals
6 feedback
7 communication

8 flowchart
9 outcomes
10 goals/objectives
11 action
12 performance
13 measure
14 alterations
15 goal-setting

Test 52

A 1 Small and Medium-sized Enterprise
   2 Boston Consulting Group
   3 Management By Objectives
   4 Management By Walking About
   5 Total Quality Management
   6 Quality in Every Single Task
   7 Return On Investment
   8 Strategic Business Unit
   9 Strengths, Weaknesses, Opportunities, Threats
   10 Computer-Aided Design
   11 Computer-Aided Manufacturing
   12 Decision Support Systems
   13 Human Resources
   14 Information Technology
   15 Just-In-Time
   16 Materials Requirement Planning
   17 Flexible Manufacturing System
   18 Break-even point
   19 Chief Executive Officer
   20 Organizational Behaviour

B 1 OB   11 IT
   2 BEP   12 SME
   3 CEO   13 ROI
   4 FMS   14 SBU
   5 MRP   15 DSS
   6 JIT   16 MBWA
   7 HR   17 SWOT
   8 QUEST   18 CAD
   9 MBO   19 CAM
   10 BCG   20 TQM

Test 53

1 profitability
2 return on investment (ROI)
3 liquidity
4 leverage
5 efficiency
6 break-even point
7 budgetary control

Test 54

1 a, b and c are all possible
2 a
3 c
4 b
5 a and c
6 b
7 a and b
8 a, b and c are all possible.

Test 55

A 1 NAFTA North American Free Trade Agreement
   2 OPEC   Organization of Petroleum Exporting Countries
   3 EU   European Union
   4 NATO   North Atlantic Treaty Organization
   5 UN   United Nations
   6 WTO   World Trade Organization
   7 WHO   World Health Organization
   8 ASEAN Association of South East Asian Nations
   9 IMF   International Monetary Fund
   10 ECB   European Central Bank
   11 FDA   (American) Food and Drug Administration
   12 OECD Organization of Economic Co-operation and Development
   13 MNCs Multinational Corporations
   14 FIFA Federation of International Football Associations

B 1 GM   General Motors
   2 IBM Intelligent Business Machines
   3 CNN Cable News Network
   4 NEC Nippon Electric Company
   5 JAL Japan Air Lines

Test 56

1 i	2 g	3 h	4 b
5 k	6 a	7 f	8 d
9 e	10 l	11 j	12 c

Test 57

A
1 language
2 cultural
3 contacts
4 transportation
5 bureaucracy
6 visas
7 residence
8 health
9 medical
10 authorities
11 tax
12 grants
13 tax
14 legal
15 duties
16 banking
17 accounts
18 currency
19 market research
20 competition
21 customers
22 promote
23 direct
24 agents
25 distributors
26 network
27 representatives
28 buy
29 rent
30 lease
31 estate
32 computer

B
1 Culture
2 Bureaucracy
3 Financial issues
4 Marketing
5 Property

Test 58*

1 multinational corporations > *trade, industrial and commercial ownership, wealth generation, investment.*
2 Internet > *communication, trade*
3 air transportation > *communication, trade*
4 defence and military alliances > *security*
5 loans to developing countries > *aid, trade, investment*
6 global warming > *environmental awareness, trade, wealth generation*

7 transnational companies > *industrial and commercial ownership, trade, investment*
8 WTO > *trade, industrial and commercial ownership, wealth generation, investment*
9 NATO > *security*
10 NAFTA > *trade, industrial and commercial ownership, wealth generation, investment*
11 UN > *everything*
12 tourism > *communication, trade, wealth generation*
13 information technology > *communication, trade, investment, industrial and commercial ownership, wealth generation*
14 share ownership > *trade, investment, industrial and commercial ownership, wealth generation*
15 global capitalism > *trade, wealth generation, investment, industrial and commercial ownership,*
16 franchise operations > *trade, investment, industrial and commercial ownership, wealth generation*
17 AIDS > *environmental awareness*
18 population growth > *environmental awareness, aid*
19 Microsoft > *trade, communication, industrial and commercial ownership, wealth generation*
20 US Supreme Court > *trade, communication, industrial and commercial ownership, wealth generation.*

* The answers given are suggested answers. The list could be longer in some cases.

Test 59

A

1 f	3 a	5 b	7 c
2 h	4 e	6 g	8 d

B
1 group-oriented culture
2 deferential culture
3 low job-mobility
4 broad-based managerial skills
5 soft, customer-focused
6 low-context culture
7 loyalty to the company
8 competitive culture

Test 60

1 c	4 j	7 b	10 e
2 f	5 a	8 k	11 d
3 g	6 i	9 h	

Word list

The numbers refer to Tests, not pages.

action 32, 38
action plan 51
administrative 47
advertising 29
advertising standards 30
advice 23
agents 57
agreement 37
aid 58
AIDS 58
alliances 23
animal rights 27, 28, 29
appendices 40
appraisal 50
artificial intelligence 48
assertiveness 20
assess 32
assets 30, 53
Association of South East Asian
  Nations (ASEAN) 55
assumptions 17
attitudes 17
audit 44
authority 17
automation 31

bank accounts 57
banking facilities 57
behaviour 7
beliefs 17
bench-marking 35, 49
bid 41
Boston Consulting Group (BCG) 46, 52
Boston Matrix 46
break-even point (BEP) 52, 53
budget 15, 38
budgetary control 53
bureaucracy 57
business culture 56
business management 38
business plan 38, 40

capacity planning 49
career path 50

cartel 26
cash cow 46
cash needs 53
ceremonies 19
change 2, 31, 35, 51
change agents 35, 37
change and communication 36
checking 32
Chief Executive Officer (CEO) 1, 52
clothing 28
collective responsibility 11
commercial ownership 58
communicating 2
communication 32, 35, 36, 51, 58
communication channels 18
company law 30
company magazine 19
comparing 2
compensation 50
competition 24, 25, 31, 57
competitive advantage 43
competitive culture 59
competitiveness 20
Computer Aided Design (CAD) 49, 52
Computer Aided Manufacturing
  (CAM) 52
Computer Integrated Manufacturing
  (CIM) 49
computers 36, 48
concession 37
confidential information 29
conflict 12
conflict management 12
consensus-minded culture 59
consumer needs 31, 43
consumer protection 28
consumers 24, 27
contacts 57
contingency plan 38
contingency theory 5
contract 15
control 52
controller 47
control process 51
controlling 2, 3, 7, 32
corporate downsizing 8
corporate strategy 44, 45

marketeers 6
marketing 6, 44, 57
Marketing Director 1
marketing plan 6, 40
marketing research 54
markets 24
Marx & Engels 5
Maslow 5, 13
Materials Requirement Planning (MRP) 49, 52
matrix structure 47
Mayo 5
measure 32, 51
measuring 42
mediation 12
medical insurance 57
meetings 36
Microsoft 58
middle management 47
mission statement 44
mobile communications 36
monitor 32, 51
monitoring 15, 51
motivation 2, 13
multinational corporations (MNCs) 56, 55, 58
myths 19

national culture 56
needs 2, 13
negotiating styles 12
negotiation 37
newsletters 36
norms 17
North American Free Trade Agreement (NAFTA) 55, 58
North Atlantic Treaty Organization (NATO) 55, 58

objectives (setting) 2, 15, 17, 38, 42, 51
operational plan 38
operations management 49
opportunities 40, 44
organization chart 47
Organization of Economic Co-operation and Development (OECD) 55
Organization of Petroleum Exporting Countries (OPEC) 55

organization 17
Organizational Behaviour (OB) 52
organizational change 35
organizational culture 17, 18, 19
organizational goals 3, 9
organizational renewal 35
organizing 2, 3, 7
outcomes 15, 51
outsourcing 8

password 48
patent 33
peer competition 23
people 6, 18
people and action plan 40
performance 51
performance monitoring 42
perks 26
personnel 47
persuasion 37
physical evidence 6
place 6
plan 16, 32
planning 2, 3, 7, 32, 37, 38, 49
politics 22, 56
population growth 58
portfolio analysis 46
power 20, 22
predict 32
preparation 37
price 6, 25
primary research 54
prioritize 16
process 6, 51
product 6
product development 54
product life cycle 33
product management 33
production 49
Production Director 1
production line 49
productivity 18, 49
profitability 53
project management 15, 41, 47
promoting 6
property 56, 57
proposals 15
public opinion 31
purchasing 49
Purchasing Director 1
purpose 17

quality 25, 43
quality circles 36
Quality in Every Single Task (QUEST) 52
quality standards 2

raw materials 24
recruitment 50
redundancies 50
redundant 43
re-engineering 8, 35
relationship building 37
relationships 13, 23
reliability 43
rent 57
representatives 57
research 32, 34, 49, 54
Research and development (R&D) 54
residence permit 57
resistance to change 35, 37
resources 3, 44, 45
retirement 50
return on investment (ROI) 52, 53
reward systems 50
rewards 19, 32
rights 26
roles 11

safety 26, 27, 28
Sale of Goods 30
sales 53
sales network 57
scheduling work 15
secondary research 54
secrets and state security 30
security 58
selling 40
sequencing and timing 41
share ownership 58
simulation 50
situations vacant 50
skills 56
skills (managerial) 59
skills audit 34
Small and Medium-Sized Enterprises (SME) 52
social legislation 30
socio-cultural factors 56

sponsorship 19
staff 47
staff development 34
Staff Development Officer 1
standards 27
start-up costs 25
status 22
stories 19
Strategic Business Unit (SBU) 46, 52
strategic management 45
strategic plan 38, 44
strategic planning 43, 46
strategy 2, 32, 42
strengths 39, 44
Strengths, Weaknesses, Opportunities, Threats (SWOT) 39, 52
structure 17
subordinates 7
supervision 2
suppliers 25, 43
sweets 29
SWOT analysis 39, 52
symbols 19
system 17
systems 18
Systems Analyst 1
Systems approach 5
systems management 47

tactical plan 38
targets 15, 42, 51
tariffs, duties and taxes 30
tax incentives 57
tax office 57
Taylorism 5
team building 2, 11
teams 7, 18, 43, 47
teamworking 8
technology 24, 31
teleconferencing 36
telephone 36
tender 15, 41
testing 28
Theory X 9
Theory Y 9
threats 39, 44
time management 2, 16
top-down culture 7
top-down management 9

Total Quality Management (TQM) 8,
   43, 52
tourism 58
trade 58
trainee 34
training 32, 34, 47, 50
training budget 34
training manager 34
transnational companies 58
transportation 56, 57, 58, 60
Trompenaars 21
turn down 16

uniforms 19
Unique Selling Proposition (USP) 6
United Nations (UN) 55, 58
upgrade 16
US Supreme Court 58

values 17, 24
video-conferencing 36
vivisection 29
voice-mail 36

waste 49
weakness 23, 39, 44
wealth 60
wealth generation 58
workforce 47
World Health Organization (WHO) 55
World Trade Organization (WTO) 55,
   58, 60

April 19/07

Bibliography

Black J. S. and Porter L.W. (2000) *Management: Meeting New Challenges.* Prentice Hall.

Crosby P. (1979) *Quality is Free.* McGraw-Hill.

Drucker P. (1968; 1985) *The Practice of Management.* Pan; Heinemann.

Hannagan T. (1998) *Management: Concepts and Practices.* Second edition. FT/Pitman Publishing.

Hofstede G. (1980) *Culture's Consequences: International Differences in Work-Related Values.* Sage Publications.

Machiavelli N. (1513) *Il Principe. (The Prince)* Penguin.

Marx K. and Engels F. (1848) *The Communist Manifesto.* Penguin.

Maslow A.H. (1942) 'A theory of human motivation' in *Psychological Review*, 50, pp. 370–96.

Maslow A.H. (1954) *Motivation and Personality.* Harper & Row.

Mayo E. (1933) *The Human Problems of an Industrial Civilisation.* Macmillan.

McGregor D. (1960) *The Human Side of Enterprise.* McGraw-Hill.

Orwell G. (1949) *Nineteen Eighty Four.* Penguin.

Peters T. and Waterman R. (1982) *In Search of Excellence.* Harper & Row.

Robbins S.P. (1996) *Organizational Behaviour.* Seventh edition. Prentice Hall International.

Schumacher E.F. (1973) *Small is Beautiful.* Abacus.

Trompenaars F. (1993) *Riding the Waves of Culture.* Nicholas Breely.